David Malouf is the internationally acclaimed author of novels and stories including *The Great World*, *Remembering Babylon*, *An Imaginary Life*, *Conversations at Curlow Creek*, *Harland's Half Acre*, *Dream Stuff*, *Every Move You Make*, *Collected Stories*, *Ransom* and the autobiographical classic *12 Edmondstone Street*. His most recent books are *A First Place*, *The Writing Life* and *Being There*. He was born in Brisbane in 1934 and lives in Sydney.

Also by David Malouf

david malouf

BOOK 2

the writing life

VINTAGE BOOKS
Australia

A Vintage book
Published by Random House Australia Pty Ltd
Level 3, 100 Pacific Highway, North Sydney NSW 2060
www.randomhouse.com.au

Penguin
Random House
Australia

First published by Knopf in 2014
This edition published in 2015

Addresses for companies within the Random House Group can be found at
www.randomhouse.com.au/offices

National Library of Australia
Cataloguing-in-Publication entry

Malouf, David, 1934– author.
The writing life/David Malouf.

ISBN 978 0 85798 407 4 (paperback)

English literature – History and criticism.
Australian literature – History and criticism.

820.9

'On Experience' reprinted with thanks to Melbourne University Press
'The Quick of Things: Lawrence and Walt Whitman' reprinted with thanks to
Sydney Review of Books
Introduction to *The Young Desire It* reprinted with thanks to Text

Cover design by Christabella Designs
Typeset in 11/17 pt Sabon by Post Pre-press Group, Brisbane
Printed in Australia by Griffin Press, an accredited ISO AS/NZS 14001:2004
Environmental Management System printer

Random House Australia uses papers that are natural, renewable and recyclable
products and made from wood grown in sustainable forests. The logging
and manufacturing processes are expected to conform to the environmental
regulations of the country of origin.

For Deborah Rogers

CONTENTS

AUTHOR'S NOTE

The pieces in this collection were produced over a period of more than forty years, some of them as articles and reviews in newspapers or magazines, others as public addresses, others again as formal introductions to classic texts. I am grateful to my various literary editors, George Munster, Paul Carter, Peter Craven and Michael Heyward, Shelley Gare and Luke Slattery, James Ley, and to the commissioning editors of the Oxford Classics, New York Review Books, the Modern Library, the Folio Society and Text. I should also thank Meredith Curnow and Patrick Mangan at Random House Australia for the care and attention they have given to bringing these pieces together so that they speak to one another in what for the reader, I hope, will be an engaging conversation.

I have dedicated the collection, with great affection, to my agent, Deborah Rogers, who died earlier this year.

WRITER AND READER

As we come together this Sunday morning at the opening of yet another Adelaide Festival Writers Week, the 22nd now in a long biennial series, it is worth asking what it is that draws so many of us back, and has done over such a long period. What do we expect of it? What do we get out of it? What should we get? And what do we mean by 'we'?

Well, writers, of course, but even more essential to the event are readers, and we are all first and foremost readers.

But let's begin with the writers – those among us who find ourselves here because we write and publish books.

If you glance about you'll recognise the writers among you from the photographs on the back of their books. You'll also see, beyond that, what you know of them, or think you know, from what you've discovered between the covers of those books; from the worlds they have created, and seduced you into entering and making your own as you follow the lure of their voice.

But already there we are talking about two different aspects of the writer. On the one hand there's the writer you see sitting over there to the left or hanging about, drink in hand, at the edge of the tent, actually present in the flesh. Who can be stared at or engaged in talk, and who, when he talks back, has opinions, some of them not at all what you might have predicted. He's been brought here in fact to do just that: to present himself through talk. He's a fair bit heavier than you imagined, and shorter, and older. She's changed her hairstyle from her last photograph. He's a bit distant – you're prepared to be generous and put it down to jetlag. She's overbright. Too eager to be liked. Already you've begun to adjust a little the image you've formed from the voice on the page. (In fact, the voice too is different from the one you heard in your head. That accent!) Because that other, imagined version of the writer is one you have made up out of your reading; out of the close relationship that has grown up over the long hours of your being closeted together, sometimes in bed, and from the special intimacy that develops between the writer's writing-self and your reading-self as you let him lead you deep into the world he is opening up; as he makes you a secret sharer in an experience that is like nothing else you have ever known. And now here he is! The man behind the voice.

Well, not quite. In fact, not at all.

*

As every writer knows, there's a gap, a mysterious and sometimes disturbing one, between the writer's daily self, his walking and talking self – the one who goes shopping or to the pub, the lover, father, ex-Marxist or lapsed Catholic who out of conscience, or as a good citizen, belongs to Amnesty International and subscribes to the Smith Family, who speaks up for the poorest and weakest among us, and against the shabby evasions of men in public office – the mistreatment, say, of refugees – and the self that gets the writing done. As there may be a difference – but I'll come back to that in just a moment – between you, each one of you, and that other agency in us that I referred to as the reading-self.

Henry James, who thought a good deal about every aspect of the writing life, and especially of the mysterious relationship between the writing-self and what I've called the walking and talking self, dramatises all this very brilliantly in one of his late short stories, 'The Private Life'.

During a house party at a Swiss hotel, the narrator is sent upstairs by an actress friend to fetch a manuscript from the room of a writer, Clare Vawdrey, who is engaged in writing a stage-piece for her. When he gets to the door of the writer's room, and knocks and enters, he is astonished to see that the desk is occupied by the writer himself, who is sitting quietly at work there in the dark. Astonished because he has just left Vawdrey, who is a very sociable character – 'loud and cheerful and copious' is how the narrator puts it – on the terrace below. When he tells his friend next day of this strange apparition, she asks what it looked like.

'It looked like the author of Vawdrey's admirable works,' he tells her. 'It looked infinitely more like him than our friend himself does.'

'Do you mean it was somebody he gets to *do* them?'

'Yes. While he dines below and disappoints you.'

'Disappoints *me*?'

'Disappoints *me*, disappoints everyone who looks in him for the genius that created the pages they adore.'

What the narrator of 'The Private Life' has discovered is an explanation at last for the gap he has always felt between the impression Vawdrey makes, his social self, which is entertaining enough but conventional – his opinions, the narrator tells us, are 'sound but second-rate' – and the admirable works.

The social self is a front, a 'dissimulation' the narrator calls it. Cover. Behind which the real writer can hide. The writer is two different people. One sits below, keeping the company 'spellbound with talk'; the

4

other is a creature of solitude, of the inner life, sitting quietly upstairs and working in the dark.

Of course it is the writer's daily self that lives the life and has the original experiences. But it is some other agency in him, what I've called the writing-self, that records them, and working in its own way, according to its own needs and in its own language, colours them with feeling, gives them resonance and meaning, so that when they come up in the writing – as the writing *calls* them up – they may be as new and surprising to the writer as they will be to the eventual reader. They have been reshaped, given a different emphasis. Transformed.

The truth is that it is the writing that shapes and leads the writer, not the other way round. The writing-self grows out of the writing and grows with it – that is what we ought to mean by a writer's 'development' – and a good deal of all this has to do with the creative action of language itself, though by language I mean something very different from the words a writer may have at his disposal for talk.

Dr Johnson tells us of his friend Oliver Goldsmith that he 'wrote like an angel and spoke like Poor Poll'. He was describing an exaggerated case of what I think is general: the gap between writing and talk, but even more the gap between the language of writing and the language of talk.

In talk, language is at the service of what needs

to be said. In writing, language is an active agent in what *gets* said. That is why writers are so wary of talk. They know that if you allow what wants to get written, what *needs* to get written, to be expressed in the serviceable language of talk, the writing will not happen. Talk will already have moved in and done the job, blocked out forever what the writing, in its own more hesitant way, was about to reveal.

So what does all that say about occasions like this?

That the writer cannot come out and present the writing-self, or that he can do it only in a teasing and unsatisfactory way. Partly because his own relationship to it is teasing and mysterious, but also because he does not need to. It has already presented itself on the page. The most he had to do is, in the vice-regal sense, *represent* it, well or badly. The best we can hope for is that when we listen to a writer reading we may catch, somewhere in the timbre of his voice, in an unusual emphasis or catch of breath, a reaffirming echo of what we have already apprehended from the page, and then go back to the page for the real thing.

So suppose we try rethinking the whole thing and consider this as a Readers Week; as an occasion where what readers come to discover is something about themselves and one another. To look about, for example, and see who it is that a particular writer has drawn together as a company; who it is that constitutes the scattered and, to the writer, unknown band, large or small, of his readers; those who, in reading, have had drawn out of them by the writing something particular and unique that tells them more clearly who they are. Mightn't we, as readers, in looking about at these others who make up that company, discover something about our own reading-self? What engages and interests it. What moves and delights it.

Reading is such a solitary activity: we can only fully respond to a book, enter into its world and allow it to uncover itself to us, by an act of the solitary self. That is why the relationship between the reader and the writer, as he exists on the page, is so intimate, so individual. But it is an experience we share with others, a whole invisible company, whose reading-selves have led them in the same direction and to the same page.

This reading-self is enticed by reading, and subtly drawn out of itself. In revealing to us the shape of our feelings, the possible life that is in the world around us, by leading us into new worlds of the imagination, what we read reshapes and changes us. What it leads us to is a future self; a self of growing perception and more complex understanding; one that is more open, more imaginative, less judgemental than our walking and talking self; one that sees in a larger way what the world might be and our own life in it. It is a self that can rise to the privilege of being the intimate, and equal, of Shakespeare, Tolstoy, Emily Brontë, Conrad, or any other writer we put ourselves, for a time, in close and challenging contact with.

Of course not all reading is of the same kind. Some reading is serious – that is, fully engaging – most reading is not. But there are books out there that in the reading of them create a richer self in us, and there exists in us this other, reading-self that is sought out by such books and appealed to, worked on, recreated; a reading-self that is not merely passively fed but which demands nourishment so that it, in turn, can nourish us.

Opening Address, Adelaide Festival
Writers Week, 2006

ON EXPERIENCE

What is it, and how do we come by it?

'EXPERIENCE DOES IT,' Mrs Micawber tells the ten-year-old David in a tearfully confidential moment in Dickens' *David Copperfield* – or, to give it its full title, *The History and Experience of David Copperfield the Younger.*

Mrs Micawber is quoting her 'dear papa', and as usual she gets it wrong. The sober and abstract *experientia docet* of the Latin, which might be rendered as 'we establish a truth by testing it', crosses the cultural barrier in poor faded Mrs Micawber's creative mishearing, as a recognition, very English and down-to-earth, of the way Life, that hard task-master, takes us by the scruff of the neck and shakes into even the most wilfully resistant of us an understanding of what it is and can do. When all the teaching and preaching and thinking and theorising in the world has failed to knock sense into our head, experience does it.

Goethe, who had a vast appetite for life, for adventures of the mind, and of the eye and heart, recommended that we should throw ourselves into experience as into an element like the sea. Generations of romantics, from Rimbaud and his contemporaries in the 1880s to the Beat poets of the 1950s and the rock-and-rollers and hippies of the 1960s, for whom intensity was all and risk served only to increase it, leapt at his advice, and a good number of them, as he warned, broke their necks. Not everyone is possessed of a Goethe's boundless vitality, his rigour and rude health and resilience.

So what is experience and how do we come by it? How much of what we experience is direct, the impinging on our senses of actual objects, phenomena, events, and how much comes in a more oblique and subliminal way? In flashes of intuition or insight. As glimpses of a reality we had not known we had hit upon till it was there in our head. Glimpses we get while we are 'looking away'. Or from whatever other-world we are in when we are asleep and dreaming, or awake and dreaming, or when our mind is idling through a task like ironing, or weeding the garden or writing; or when we are absorbed in the wordless, thoughtless, unbodied world of music.

There is a moment early on in *David Copperfield* when young David, on one of his visits to the Micawbers in the King's Bench Prison, is sent upstairs to borrow a knife and fork from another inmate, Captain Hopkins. When he comes away it is with more than he was sent for:

> Captain Hopkins lent me the knife and fork with compliments to Mrs Micawber. There was a very dirty lady in his room and two wan girls, his daughters with shock heads of hair. I thought it was better to borrow Captain Hopkins' knife and fork than Captain Hopkins' comb. The Captain himself was in the last extremity of shabbiness, with large whiskers, and an old brown greatcoat with no other coat below it. I saw his bed rolled up in a corner; and what plates and dishes and pots he had, on a shelf; and divined (God knows how) that though the two girls with shock heads were Captain Hopkins' children, the dirty lady was not married to Captain Hopkins. My timid station on the threshold was not occupied more than a couple of minutes at the most; but I came down again with all this in my knowledge, as surely as the knife and fork were in my hand.

This is an exemplary passage. Everything in it is relevant to the moment of insight or vision, to the mere glimpse that by some mysterious process (God knows how) becomes knowledge, becomes experience: the 'threshold' – which is not so much a crossing point to a further room as to a further mind space; the observer's 'timid station' there – a state of passive receptivity in which intuition works in no time at all, 'a couple of minutes at most', so that what the eye records (the shock heads of the girls, the dishes and pots on the shelf) and what he 'sees' (that sudden apprehension) are of the same consistency, and both have the reality and substance of what can be held in the hand.

The older David Copperfield who is recalling this is a writer, and his younger counterpart works like the writer he will become. Writers have a particular interest in experience and how we come by what we 'know'; how, in the light of it, we may teach ourselves to act more wisely, or more cautiously or with a greater awareness of the consequences of what we do; how to deal with what life and living does to us. In this, writers are not much different from anyone else, but because of the work they do may be more self-examining and enquiring than the average man, more inward and analytical; and none so subtle, or with a more scrupulous appreciation of the distinctions and mysteries of the business, than Henry James.

In a famous essay on *The Art of Fiction*, James, in accepting the proposition that 'one must write from experience', goes on to ask: 'What kind of experience is intended, and where does it begin and end? Experience,' he insists, 'is never limited and it is never complete; it is an immense sensibility, a kind of huge spider's web of the finest silken threads suspended in

12

the chamber of consciousness, and catching every airborne particle in its tissue. It is the very atmosphere of the mind.'

It is important to see what James is suggesting here. Experience as he conceives it is more than an accumulation of informative occasions or interesting facts or perceptions, or of real happenings encountered by the self as it moves through place and time. It is a capacity to respond to what the world presents us with; to absorb, to register; and this capacity will be great or little according to each one of us. So he can go on, 'When the mind is imaginative – much more when it happens to be that of a man of genius – it takes to itself the faintest hints of life, and converts the very pulses of the air into revelations.'

He then makes a very bold claim that has to do with the seeming limitations that might be involved in the demand that 'we write from what we know'. Taking an extreme case, he tells us:

> The young lady living in a village has only to be a damsel upon whom nothing is ever lost to make it quite unfair (as it seems to me) to declare to her that she shall have nothing to say about the military. Greater miracles have been seen than that, imagination assisting, she should speak the truth about some of these gentlemen.

What James is allowing for is the existence in us of a quality well beyond the ordinary (imagination, but also the capacity to make much of little) that might allow his observant young lady access to a world she would appear, given her sex and position, to have no useful knowledge of: and he offers as evidence a startling example:

> I remember an English novelist, a woman of genius, telling me that she was much commended for the impression she had managed to give in one of her tales of the nature and way of life of the French Protestant youth. She had been asked where she had learned so much about this recondite being, she had been congratulated on her peculiar opportunities. The opportunities consisted in her once, in Paris, as she ascended a staircase, passed an open door where, in the household of a *pasteur*, some of the young Protestants were seated at a table round a finished meal. The glimpse made a picture; it lasted only a moment, but the moment was experience.

This mirrors in a quite remarkable way the circumstances of young David Copperfield at the door to Captain Hopkins' room. The same 'threshold' situation, the same apprehension, in a single moment, of all that is needed for a 'glimpse' to expand and become knowledge. But James takes us a step further.

His woman of genius, he tells us, 'was blessed with the faculty which when you give it an inch takes an ell ... the power to guess the unseen from the seen, to trace the implication of things, to judge the whole by the pattern, the condition of feeling life in general so completely that you are well on the way to knowing any corner of it ... If experience consists of impressions, it may well be said that impressions *are* experience.'

Of course not all experience consists of what James calls impressions. Much of it comes to us in direct dealings with the world of events and accidents, the irruption into our lives of obstacles, some of them larger than we can manage, or fatally destructive, that we have to negotiate as best we can. What James is arguing for is the inner view, the sort of knowledge that comes, as it does to young David Copperfield at the door to Captain Hopkins' room, as if from nowhere, and which most of us, if we are consciously aware of it, barely question. The writer is different only in that he is especially responsive to such impressions. That is his temperament, the very 'atmosphere of the mind', James would say, that he moves in.

And we might go a step further here, and ask ourselves if what we call experience doesn't also consist of impressions that come to us, not 'from God knows where' but from a place equally mysterious and off the map, the imagination.

I'm thinking of occasions when our mind plays a peculiar trick on us and memory hits on an event so real, so alive in every way to our senses, that we take it at first for the recall of something that actually happened to us; we are so keenly aware of what it felt like to be there at the centre of it – the way the light fell, the very quality of the surrounding air. Then we think again. This isn't something that happened to us. It's something we read in a book! – But didn't that also happen? How else explain the certainty we felt of having been there in our actual body; at an occasion, imaginary as it was, that had all the immediacy of sensory impact and presence with which real events come to us?

The truth is that the thing did happen, but to our *reading-self*, while we were lost as we say in a book. And isn't that precisely what we read for? Or go to the theatre or the opera or the movies for? This experience of being both there and not there. There in our real body, but more powerfully as well in some other, more mysterious entity; a disembodied mind or consciousness that is free to move beyond itself into new and finer, or more dangerous or painful situations, and emerge not only unscathed, but re-energised, enlivened.

This surely is one of our most ancient pleasures. From the earliest days of storytelling, round the campfire or in the marketplace or in halls where the great epics and sagas were recited, this must have been the attraction, intensely personal, hugely liberating, that drew us to sit quietly in company, yet at the same time alone, and give ourselves up to entranced, excited *listening*. Especially in societies that were not yet literate and where storytelling was one of the few communal entertainments.

Entering a story – a fairytale or folk-tale or fable: being taken out of ourselves into the skin of another; having adventures there that are both our own and not our own – is an experience of a particular kind. Release from the constrictions, whatever they may be, of our own life and body into a dimension where reality is not limited to dailiness and the laws of nature, and all sorts of occasions, richer and more fantastic, more exciting, more harrowing, can be imaged forth – *imagined* – and made real. There is a regenerative and healing quality here that makes such experiences something more than entertainment or simply a way of passing the time; though the passing of time is also essential to it.

Time in a story passes more quickly than in real life – 'the next day' we say, all in a breath, or 'some years later'. But it may also pass more slowly, or stop altogether, giving the narrator, and the listener, the luxury of looking around and absorbing things that in real life are gone too quickly to be taken in, or to consider and ask questions that real life leaves no space for. Such games offer a momentary respite from calendar and body time into the free time of 'ever after'. As if by losing ourselves in the story, we had, at least for its duration, stopped the body's clock from ticking on inevitably to death, and escaped its laws and limitations. Could, for example, be in several places at the same time, or slip out of one body into another, or put off the conditions of our heavy earth-bound nature and fly.

This is the experience we get these days, the experience we seek, from reading, and the effect is all the stronger because of the solitary and inward nature of that activity, the complex alternation of active and passive attention it demands.

We take this, and our easy adaption to it, so much for granted that it is difficult to imagine a state in which these reading-selves of ours had not yet emerged; as it is difficult for us to imagine any other self than the one we now live with, or to believe, perhaps, that a pre-literate self, inhabiting a pre-literate world, though it experienced things in a very different way, might have been no less complex, and possessed of a sensibility no less rich and crowded with sensations, than the one that now lives daily with motor vehicles, super-markets, mobile phones, and an information system that has access to satellites, out there in *space*, that beam into our homes and offices – but instantane-ously – what is still in process of occurring on the far side of the globe.

It takes a strong exercise of the imagination, of *un*-remembering, of emptying our minds (our bodies too with their accustomed reflexes) of all they know and take for granted, to see how differently men and women of another age might have come at the world. We need to run the mind backwards like a film, letting it discard as it goes all acquaintance with those means by which, over more than two centuries now, information has come pouring into our overloaded sensory systems – email, the internet, the mobile phone, the computer, the fax machine; then television, radio, the telephone, the telegraph; finally newspapers, periodicals, the printed book – till we find ourselves back once more at a point where news comes to us by word of mouth and slowly, at pony or walking pace; a time before rail or motor transport when even a journey to the next village was a venture seriously undertaken, and news was what was happening a dozen miles, not half a planet away.

What we call consciousness must have had a different feel then, and bodies too; when everything that came to hand came first hand, out of a world that was always within reach, and for the most part only in reach; when to make any discovery at all of what surged and spawned and swarmed around you, of how things worked, you had to be all eyes and ears for the immediate detail and effect, since your only source of knowledge was looking and listening. Looking closely and giving yourself time to take in the smallest deviations and differences. Listening. Listening *in*.

Of course there must have been observers and observers, and that quality of imagination that allows some men and women to build on what they have observed; and intuitions that could take some of them 'beyond'. There must also have been degrees of listening, of catching more than the next man of what was being said. And there must have been those as well in whom the link between eye and mind, eye and hand, was unusually quick.

We know from the sermons that have come down to us from the sixteenth and early seventeenth century, when much of normal Sunday churchgoing had to do with hour-long addresses from the pulpit, what practised listeners these churchgoers must have been; from speeches too in the theatre, where what had originally been a crowd in search of crude sensation and knockabout farce had, in little more than two decades, become an 'audience' that could follow the complex moral arguments and riddling wordplay of a Hamlet, a Macbeth, a Lear. This, if nothing else, should convince us that the pre-literate, or mixed literate and pre-literate world that makes up so much of human history was neither undeveloped nor primitive. There are places all over the planet, even now, in an age of instant information and global consciousness, where a highly advanced technology and low literacy exist side by side; so that men and women living in the same space, and in daily contact, draw their experience simultaneously from different sources. Directly, in the age-old way of observing and listening, and in addition to this, if they are literate, through whatever advanced technology is available to them. And if we take the long view, this 'mixed' set of conditions, where the two forms of experience exist side by side, is the norm.

This is how it was in the classical world of Plato and Aristotle and the Greek dramatists, of Vergil and Plutarch and Horace; in the world of Dante and Petrarch and Shakespeare; and as it is in many places today. It is worth recalling, when we are tempted to be complacent about our own high level of development, that the greatest works of philosophy and literature, before the eighteenth century, were produced in societies that were largely illiterate, though not necessarily uneducated in the wider sense, and that the scientific discoveries that have made the largest contribution to life on our planet – the making of fire, the domestication of seeds and animals, and of fruit and vegetables by cross-breeding or grafting, the irrigation and fertilisation of soils – were the work not of trained scientists, but through long centuries of observing and experimenting in a purely practical way, or through a sudden leap of the imagination, or by making an inspired guess and getting it right, of humble herders and farmers, and in some places, such as Africa and South America, of women.

It is the richness of such 'mixed' worlds as a source of individual experience that answers what has for so long been a problem to some of our best scholars and commentators: how it is that a youth growing up in a town of some fifteen hundred souls, and with little more in the way of education than seven or eight years at the local grammar school, could have acquired the wealth of knowledge, and the experience, across so many trades and professions and orders of society, that is on show in the plays that come to us under the name of William Shakespeare.

Quite apart from the question of how much formal education a writer might actually need (think of Dickens), what this problem ignores is that other quality Henry James points to, 'the faculty which when you give it an inch takes an ell'.

That 'inch', in the young Shakespeare's case, was a prosperous town with a wide range of home-based industries – brewing, weaving, tanning, dyeing (Shakespeare's father was a glover) – as well as all the trades associated with building, and in close proximity to a countryside of orchards, 'small pelting farms' and larger ones involved in the many branches of the wool trade.

Should we really assume that to have access to all he 'knew' – that inside knowledge the plays reveal of the law, of drugs, cures, seamanship, and a very convincing expertise in such military matters as the laying of mines and the conducting of sieges – the young Shakespeare must at some time have been articled, or practised medicine, or been to sea, or done service on one of Elizabeth's many military adventures on the continent? All this a young man with an ear for shop-talk and an eye for observing workmen at their trade, especially a young person of imagination and genius as James puts it, on whom nothing was ever lost, could have picked up – with no awareness as yet that he was in training for his own barely existent trade – in the streets of Stratford itself, or in the houses of neighbours, or in idle hours at a tavern in the company of some sailor home from the sea or soldier back from the wars.

The range of what Shakespeare acquired in the way of experience was prodigious; he was, after all, a prodigy. But the means by which he came to it was common, and is so still.

Young people today grow up in a world where information comes to them through sophisticated high-tech systems – the internet, email, iPads – and where communication across a wide range of places and persons is both frequent and immediate. Space and time have been telescoped, intimacy replaced by a new kind of distance; and this is just one example of a distancing that has become general in the culture as a whole. Our global economy means that commodities and products that were once local or seasonal are now available everywhere in the developed world and at all times of the year; but this also sets us at a remove, personally, from all but the most abstract acquaintance with their source and production. Everything now, from fruit and vegetables of the most exotic kind to eggs, chicken thighs, cereals, comes packaged or frozen, in a way that makes invisible, and to many young people unimaginable and of no interest or concern, the natural world to which these things once belonged and the skills of those who produce and gather them. In the case of a plastic tray of chops, for example, the long process from breeding to slaughter that was once the life of a real animal and has brought it first to the supermarket, now to the table.

A continuity has been broken. Between the part of our experience that sets us in nature, as one of its creatures and subject to its laws and changes, and that other part where we exist as social and economic units, consumers. What has got lost in the break is much that once belonged to our direct sensory experience – the glow of a ripe peach behind leaves, the first blades of green in a furrow, the feel under our hand of the bristles on the back of a hog, the dance of threads in a hand-loom; something too (think of what fed so much poetry) of our sense of the world we were in as a place of teeming variety and growth, in which each thing had its moment of perfected ripeness or growth, but also, inevitably, of decline, and was a source of *feeling* in us as well as of use.

The change in most places, and in the lives of many of us who are still living, has been rapid. Even fifty years ago, a child growing up in a good-sized town, as I did in Brisbane in the forties and fifties, would have had a backyard to play in, with two or three pawpaw trees and a mango or lemon, rows of peas, beans, tomatoes, onions, lettuce, a corner for rhubarb where fat snails congregated, and a chook-house where you could reach your hand in and feel for the warmth of a new-laid egg. Also, close beside it, a block where some familiar rooster or hen had its head chopped off for Sunday dinner, and afterwards hung from a hook trailing threads of sticky gore, headless but still convulsively flapping its wings.

All this is gone in most city places, and with it the baker's boy with his basket of warm loaves, the milkman's horse clopping down the street just before dawn, the milk in a striped jug on the front step, covered with a doily weighted with beads.

But that said, there is something still of that older way of experiencing things that is not gone. Families, for all the changes, remain pretty much what they have always been: little word-of-mouth societies, repositories of facts, skills, stories, teasing secrets (and sometimes insoluble mysteries), where children pick up what they first know of the world in the way they always have, by question and answer. By puzzling things out from what they are told – but more often from what they are not told but gather by eavesdropping, or like the young David Copperfield, by lingering on a threshold to catch what comes to them, in a flash, from God knows where, or as a glimpse while they are 'looking away'.

Children continue, even in an age of technology, to acquire a good deal of what they will one day think of as their first experience in the most old-fashioned ways. Through codes, habits, rituals – which provide us with our first apprehension of how things fit together to make a style of living or local culture; how power works and who has it and how it can be negotiated – how it can be manipulated too and misused; who among those who come and go in a household belong, and to what degree, and who does not and why; all the ins and outs of family lore and gossip that no-one sets out precisely to inform us of but which we take in and carry with us for the rest of our days.

This, in the making of young lives, is much, and not to be underestimated. What is being shaped here, as the questions arise and are provisionally answered, is a take on the world that will be conditional, as all experience is, on the disposition of the little watcher and listener, and in that way tempered to the purely personal view. 'We cannot say too little,' Emerson warns, 'of our constitutional necessity of seeing things under private aspects, or saturated with our humours.' Much more will come, as a life gathers the elements that will define it: love, loss, a vocation discovered and professional skills acquired, partnership, parenthood, perhaps a time at war – the thousand oddities of experience undergone and accidents survived. But what these amplify and build on is what has already been laid down in those first months and years, and was acquired in the most traditional way.

A child learns early how to pick up the facts he needs to make sense of the world and make a 'story' of it – *his* story. In the word-of-mouth world that is a family, storytelling is still part of the complex give and take of daily intercourse, a means of weaving the past into the present to create continuity, of holding the adult storyteller and the little wide-eyed listener in a single moment and on a single breath. Here children keep touch, through story, with their own past lives, and get living glimpses, as much through what a voice carries of feeling as through word-pictures or facts, into the lives of their parents and grandparents. Such formulae as 'Tell me the time when' renew a child's contact with the reassuringly familiar, but always in the hope that this time round some new detail will emerge and give the story a different colour or dimension, or that he himself will catch something in it that he missed in other tellings and will this time take him 'beyond'.

The truth is that our experience, for all that we are the subject of it, is a mystery to us. We have no notion, amid the events and feelings and words and pictures that crowd in upon us, of the advent of our most secret understandings, the moments that will one day mean most to us, which image glimpsed, or word spoken, will occasion in us that sweet shock in which the whole 'spider's web of the finest silken threads', to go back to Henry James' image, will suddenly glow and tremble in the chamber of our consciousness.

'We do not know today,' Emerson tells us in a memorable passage, 'whether we are busy or idle. In times when we thought ourselves indolent, we have discovered afterwards that much was accomplished, and much was begun in us. All our days are so uncomfortable while they pass, that 'tis wonderful where or when we ever got anything of this thing which we call wisdom, poetry, virtue. We never got it on any dated calendar day. Some heavenly days must have been intercalated somewhere, like those that Hermes won with dice of the Moon, that Osiris might be born.'

WHEN THE WRITER SPEAKS

THE REAL ENEMY OF writing is talk. There is something about the facility of talk, the ease with which ideas clothe themselves in the first available words, that is antithetical to the way a writer's mind works when he is engaged in the slower, and, one wants to say deeper business of writing. And of course once the words have come in one form it is more difficult to discover them in another. The voice of easy speaking has already occupied the space that needs to be filled by that quieter, more interior, less sociable voice that belongs to solitude and to waiting – to waiting patiently for the writing itself to speak. That is why writers are so unwilling to talk about work in progress. They are afraid of speaking too soon and from the wrong place, with the wrong voice; of resolving too quickly, in talk, the tension whose energies they will need to draw on later, in solitary struggle and against the resistance of what has not yet been articulated. The writer needs both to trust words and to be wary of them. A writer, as Thomas Mann tells us, is someone who finds writing difficult.

Silence: that is the natural state from which writing proceeds; a state in which the voice in our head, which only very reluctantly ceases to argue and assert, to hold forth on what it knows or to mull over old occasions and slights and controversies, falls still at last and allows that other, smaller voice to be heard that knows nothing of 'issues', has no opinions or convictions, is curious, doubtful, and interested in *everything*, eager to live inside each thing and to discover and recreate, so far as language allows, the life that is in it.

The writer I have been evoking is what we loosely call the imaginative writer, the poet, the teller of tales whose business, as he would see it, is with discovery; not the articulation of some previously held view but the groping through words towards something only vaguely grasped and which he will recognise only when words have set it down on the page.

There is, of course, another kind of writing, and if I make a distinction between the two it is not to create a hierarchy but to suggest that they are products of different states of consciousness.

This other form of writing does belong to the world of moral or social or political issues; to argument, opinion, judgement. It is the product of a consciousness that is very active and alert and it needs these qualities to do what it must do, which is to challenge, question, turn received ideas on their heads; and the more it knows, and the more, at the very moment of writing, it can draw on what it knows, the richer the writing will be, the more focused, the more wide-ranging and convincing.

This argumentative or expository sort of writing is too varied to have a single name. It would have to be a very loose term indeed that would contain say, Milton's *Areopagitica* and the pamphlets on divorce, Johnson's *Lives of the Poets*, Tom Paine and Burke, Thoreau's 'On Civil Disobedience', Hazlitt and Emerson's essays, Shaw's musical criticism under the name of Cornetto di Basso, or such contemporary examples as the work of Janet Malcolm and Julian Barnes' pieces for *The New Yorker*. The point of distinction, as I say, is not quality but the different attitudes of mind out of which the two forms of writing are produced. One is active and supremely self-conscious, grounded in reason but open to the spirit of play; the other, in the Keatsian sense, deeply passive, where the less conscious you are of what you already know, the more of previous knowledge, and the attitudes and opinions that go with it, has fallen out of your head, the more responsive you will be to what the writing itself is about to discover, the readier you will be to get on with the real business of attending – in both senses – on what you are about to be told.

The novel, which for the past 150 years or so has been the major literary form in our culture, is an interesting case because it is mixed.

In earlier novels, Hugo's *Notre-Dame* for instance, or *Moby-Dick*, the two forms of writing may both be present but are kept distinct. The essayistic chapters that interrupt and expand the narrative in *Notre-Dame* are brilliantly argumentative, full of dazzlingly original speculations on the relationship between language and architecture – the idea, for instance, in the chapter called 'Ceci Tuera Cela' that the printing-press killed architecture – or on the social changes behind different architectural styles. But however playful and imaginative they may be, however full of poetic flare, these chapters belong to a different mode, a different form of thinking, from the bold language-act by which Hugo appropriates a neglected and half-ruined building and raises it out of the realm of stone into that of language, makes of it a verbal artefact, a text that is literally written all over with multilingual graffiti, or from the descent into the world of folk-tale, and dream or nightmare, that creates Quasimodo as a living extension of the cathedral, one of its gargoyles made flesh. And we might make the same distinction between the various parts of *Moby-Dick*, where the essays on every aspect of whaling – precise, poetic, self-consciously playful, sceptical and subversive even, in the manner of the French Encyclopaedists – belong to a different world of invention from that of Ahab and the others, which dives down deep into a form of poetic thinking that is continuous with dreaming, and demands a different and more 'poetic', that is allusive and reverberative, language.

A century later this essayistic quality gets integrated into the main narrative, and Thomas Mann, for instance, goes to considerable lengths to insist that the philosophical arguments and political exchanges in *The Magic Mountain* are as much a product of the poetic spirit as the complex imagery of disease that makes the rest of the book so clearly a work of the imagination.

Mann recognises a crisis here. What he has to say about the novel reflects on his own position in the earlier part of the last century but points to something generally true that we need to take account of. The novel, he tells us, 'because of its analytical spirit, its consciousness, its innate critical attitudes, can no longer remain undisturbed and sweetly oblivious of the world'.

That 'no longer' suggests that the situation is new, and in some ways it is. Mann is speaking of an age in which the novelist too, as he sees it, 'can no longer remain undisturbed and sweetly oblivious of the world'.

*

Mann had not always taken this line. Before he began the long investigation of his social and aesthetic attitudes that he called *Reflections of an Unpolitical Man*, which kept him occupied for four whole years from September 1914 till the end of the war, he would have taken it for granted that his purely imaginative work, *Death in Venice*, say, or *Tristan*, stood apart from his political writings and that 'to think and judge humanly is to think and judge unpolitically'. But the events of those years, and the writing of the book, changed him. When he began he was a conservative nationalist, anti-democratic in the tradition of Schopenhauer and Nietzsche. Too much the 'writer', that is, too eager to live in contraries and contradictions, too ironical, too aware of the need to qualify, to be a true polemicist, Mann found himself, as he emerged from his four-year ordeal and transformation, no longer on one side of the political line but on the other, a social democrat no less, and a committed supporter of the new republic. By the mid-thirties he could claim that he did not 'rank the socio-political sphere lower than that of the inner life'.

This business of the writer discovering, as he writes, what he really thinks, which may run counter to what he *believes* he thinks, comes close to the heart of what I want to say.

This is when the writer speaks: out of his activity as a writer rather than as a good citizen or as a holder of this or that set of views. What he finds himself saying then may surprise and even shock him – and the writing will please him most perhaps when it does. It will be his assurance that a real act of writing has occurred. But it can happen only if he is prepared to go lax and empty. To give up what he *thinks* he knows and allows some other faculty to take over. Hugo may have been the earliest writer to recognise this phenomenon and put it into words. 'All great writers,' he tells us, 'create two *oeuvres*, one deliberate, the other involuntary.' And again: 'As a person, one is sometimes a stranger to what one writes as a poet.'

Hugo's first proposition is wonderfully illustrated in his great contemporary Balzac. Balzac was by conviction a conservative. Catholic and Royalist, he speaks with contempt, even as late as the revolutionary year of 1848, in the preface to his last-published book, *The Peasants*, of 'the democratic vertigo to which so many blind writers succumb'. He must have despised the woolly liberalism and drum-banging about Progress, and the sentimentality about peasants and workers (Balzac actually knew his peasants) that is at the damp centre of Hugo's writing.

But what the books themselves dramatise is not a right-wing view, or any view at all in that sense, but a series of radical insights into a phenomenon that Balzac found more fascinating than any other and which he approaches with the excited detachment of the naturalist who has discovered another form of Nature, nineteenth-century entrepreneurial capitalism; the way it corrupts private and public values, divides families, hardens the heart, and makes of the mind an instrument that can be deadly in its excessiveness and blind determination. The drive to success, the beating down of others in order to prevail – that is what animates Balzac's characters, and, as a writer, living in the phenomenon as he observes and recreates it, what animates *him*. Even sex is either something to be manipulated and traded, or money-making becomes the expression of sexual energy in another form. The Market, whose working for Balzac is like the mysterious working of the universe, is a machine in which all his characters are caught, a contemporary version of what older writers, and writers like Hugo, called Fate, or Providence.

It is as if these novels were written by the left hand of a man whose convictions they entirely violate. Even his own religious affiliations are not sacred. In one of the finest comic scenes he ever wrote, Madame Marneffe in *Cousin Bette* does a devastating imitation of poor Baroness Hulot's virtuous piety as she pleads for mercy from her seducer Crevel, and the malicious delight Balzac takes in it, the energy it generates in him, is impersonal, has nothing to do with his own loyalties, and allows nothing to the fact that Baroness Hulot is genuinely virtuous and also helpless. He enters fully into the comic inventiveness of his creation, Madame Marneffe, and exploits it with a savagery that even Diderot, at his most anti-clerical, does not match.

What we see here is that joy in the phenomenon itself, for its own sake and outside moral judgement, that is the true characteristic of the artist: a delight in God's creation but also in his own. To enter, in a spirit of exuberant play, into even what is reprehensible – that is the artist's way; which is why satirists so often get into trouble for loving too clearly what they excoriate. But what else should they do? Delight in the thing itself, the taking into yourself of its energy, the giving of your own energy to the free expression of it, the letting it run its course – that is what constitutes the artist's interest in things; in the *otherness* of things. Outside the work he might take a stand; but in so far as he does it inside the work, even if it is on the side of the angels, by so much the less is he an artist. The work as a delighting of the spirit in *what is* has nothing to do with consciousness-raising, or progress, or right religion or right thinking. Chaucer may make a deathbed renunciation of his works on the grounds of their immorality, their impiety, and poor Isaac Babel in the Lubianka his on the grounds of political incorrectness, but the works, in all their lively incorrectness, shine clear.

Of course one can argue that there are more

important things than art. But they are not what concern the writer while he is writing. If he wants to put his work at the service of a cause, that's his choice. Time will make its own judgement, both on the cause and his attachment to it. When the writer speaks, when he most truly speaks, is when he allows the writing to speak.

But given Mann's statement that the novel, and by implication the novelist too, 'can no longer remain undisturbed and sweetly oblivious of the world', when should the writer speak up, speak out *in propria persona*, as a citizen, but also, unavoidably in his case, as one who comes invested with whatever authority the writing itself has won for him?

Some writers, on some occasions, have always done so: Voltaire for example, when he took up the case of Calas, Zola when, in *J'accuse*, he spoke out in the Dreyfus affair; most of all Hugo who in his attack on Louis Napoleon in *Napoléon le Petit*, set himself up as the embodiment of an alternative France, the president in exile of a republic of the spirit that was the *true* France – and it is worth noting perhaps that all three cases are French.

Hugo was also the first writer after Voltaire to have a universal celebrity – almost separate from his fame as a writer but growing out of it – that gave his name, on any petition, in any cause, real currency from Mexico to Vietnam. His is the earliest example of a phenomenon that has now become general; in which writers, in a world where virtually everything has been subsumed into the culture of advertising, are asked increasingly, like those fake housewives who used to promote the virtues of washing-powder on TV, to endorse anything that needs for its selling that little extra push; from one another's books to every sort of appeal for funds or the support of this or that political party at an election, but also in protest against the horrors that, despite old Hugo's optimism, show no sign of going away.

Thomas Mann is perhaps the most significant example in our time of a writer drawn out of his role as pure writer into that of public adversary; driven to speak up, out of what he called the 'spiritual confusion' of his time, for reason, justice, humanity, but most of all for that humane culture without which these cannot be sustained.

One of Mann's most moving statements is one he made in 1931 in answer to a question from young people about how, in a period of intense political struggle, one could go on writing. We do it, Mann answered, 'because we believe in play and its dignity. We believe in secrets, in the human secret of art.'

What makes the statement so moving is that Mann is speaking up for what is deeply personal, for what is closest to his heart, and to the centre of his private world, at a moment when he is already moving, or being moved, on to the public stage: as the figurehead of the 'other Germany', much as Hugo had been of the 'other France'.

It was a role he accepted very unwillingly and after a good deal of vacillation; he knew in advance what it would cost him. Speaking in a diary entry of 1933 of the defection to the Nazis of the grand old man of German letters, Gerhart Hauptmann, he writes: 'I hate this idol whom I helped to magnify, and who magnificently regrets a martyrdom that I also feel I was not born for, but which I am driven to embrace for the sake of intellectual integrity.'

What tormented Mann was the fear that a role that had been forced upon him by an accident of history might also have driven him out of what he had always seen as his natural course: the one that 'large-handed Nature' had offered him, like Goethe, as one of her favoured sons. In a diary entry of March 1934, he writes: 'The inner rejection of martyrdom, the feeling that it is not appropriate for me, continues to be strong. Just now it has been re-awakened, and was confirmed and reinforced, when Lion quoted a remark made by Gottfried Benn a long time ago, "Do you know Thomas Mann's house in Munich? There is truly something Goethean about it" – The fact that I was driven away from that existence is a serious flaw in the destined pattern of my life, one which I am attempting to accommodate to – in vain, it appears; and the impossibility of setting it right, and re-establishing that existence, impresses itself upon me, no matter how I look at it, and gnaws at my heart.'

What these private diary entries reveal is how unnatural it is for the artist to enter the world of political action and to speak *there* rather than in his own place on the stillness of the page. Mann is deeply torn; his reactions, from day to day, are contradictory, he wants to save himself from all this. He does speak out at last, but, being Mann, is also aware of the irony of his position; of the unpolitical man's having become after all, as he puts it, 'an itinerant preacher for democracy – a role whose comic element was always plain'.

But irony does not diminish in any way either the energy he expended in his fight against Nazism or his courage. It cost him many years of exile and his natural audience, the one that over more than thirty years he had made his own, and the right to publish in his homeland. It is only because he was such an indefatigable worker and had such a strong sense of his own destiny as writer, because he needed so much to hang on to his 'secrets', to the 'dignity of play', that it did not cost him as well some of the greatest of his works.

The Goethe book, *Lotte in Weimar*, and the four Joseph novels, are not only a marvellous expression of culture as he understood it – and all the more since they were made in defiance of the absolute challenge to it – but a tribute as well to his powers of dedication and belief. It is they, with their essential lightness, their freedom from taint, rather than his political activities, that stand as a counterweight to the brutalities of the period and so triumphantly outlast them.

Mann had always written articles on social and political matters. However much he protested the opposite, he was at home with controversy. He also saw himself, in a very German way, as 'representative' – the idea has no equivalent in our literary culture; no writer in English has ever presented himself, I think, as the personification of the language and the living embodiment, for his time, of all that can best be said in it. Mann had always been in the public eye. He orchestrated his reputation, enjoyed his fame, and enjoyed even more when it came – from America of course – his celebrity; and it was his celebrity that had to be exploited when he came to fulfil his role as the good German, since its main target was political opinion in the United States. I say this not to diminish the part he played but to suggest how many-sided it was, and the ways in which the use of it, the usefulness of it, was not always in his control.

Given the way Mann saw things, he could have done nothing else. But there were others and they acted differently. One of them was the poet Gottfried Benn, the same poet we have just seen Mann referring to in his diary.

Another unpolitical man, Benn was one of the leading voices of pre-Nazi Germany, an expressionist, a Francophile, insistent always that poetry existed in its own world, free of the sociopolitical. But in a famous broadcast of 1933 he supported the election of the Nazis, and as vice-president of the writers' wing of the Prussian Academy drafted the declaration that all German writers were asked to make giving their unconditional support, with a simple yes or no, to the new regime – incidentally, the answer Mann gave was deliberately ambiguous, and it was to be another three years before he made his final break with his homeland. Benn meanwhile, within the year in fact, had seen his error, and while Mann was still being published in Germany was expelled from all his official positions and forbidden to work professionally, either in medicine (he was a skin specialist) or literature.

Early on in the regime he had written a letter of challenge to the *émigrés*, especially those, like Heinrich Mann, who were not Jewish. Now he did not leave Germany and join them but went into what he called an inner emigration: silence. He joined the army, put himself at the service of German soldiers on the Eastern Front, wrote only for himself, and did not publish again until 1948. He was choosing to share with his fellow Germans an experience he felt he could not walk away from because they could not.

In the writer's way of being always in at least two

minds, I find it hard to choose between these very different ways of responding to an impossible situation: the one acting up to an international audience, a courageous speaking out, and making himself endlessly available for comment, of a man who wanted nothing more than to be allowed to get on with his own writing, but who recognised a solemn public duty; in Benn's case an acceptance, out of sight of all witnesses but himself, of a silence he could only hope would be temporary, and a dedication, in the meantime, to the physical suffering of men whose life and fate, inside the historical moment, he felt it was his duty to share.

Like a good many writers, I suspect, who have spent their whole lives on the light side of history, I am haunted by the lives of those who have found themselves in darker places and in darker times. By that no doubt terrifying phone-call from Stalin, for example, that left Pasternak unable to find the few words in support of a fellow poet that might have saved Mandelstam from deportation to Siberia and an anonymous death. By the situation Camus found himself in at the height of the Algerian war. By the different paths taken in the Nazi period by Mann and Benn.

At a time when everything, including even what we used to call history, has become spectacle, an extension of the twenty-four hour news cycle, we might have to resist the recruiting of our support – which means our name and whatever may have accrued to it as 'recognition value' – in any but the most serious causes. The expression of opinion, which is a slippery enough commodity anyway, is just another form of self-presentation, a temptation to talk – and trivial talk – that is, as I said at the beginning, the real enemy of writers, and all the more tempting in this case because it flatters with the assurance of public importance, and because real or whipped-up energy, in the overheated world of the media, can seem such a reassurance of *presence*.

The writer is most present in the writing itself; which is a product of silence. We are luckiest, as writers, if the society we live in allows us the privilege of silence. But one that is chosen, not enforced.

Annual address to English PEN, London, 1998

'THE MOST BEAUTIFUL AND PUREST MIRROR'

TOTAL WAR AND GENOCIDE are not modern concepts. Early on in the *Iliad*, Menelaus, Helen's deserted husband, captures a rich Trojan, Adrestus, and is tempted to accept a ransom and spare his life. His brother Agamemnon, the Greek leader, is furious: 'Did the Trojans treat you so handsomely when they were your guests? No, we are not going to leave a single one of them alive, down to the babies in their mother's wombs – not even they must live. The whole people must be wiped from existence, and none be left to remember them and shed a tear.'

Only Achilles, in his hatred of the other Greeks after his quarrel with Agamemnon, is more extreme. 'How happy I should be,' he tells Patroclus, 'if not a Trojan got away alive, not one, and not an Argive either, and we two alone survived to pull down Troy's diadem of towers, single-handed.'

*

The *Iliad* has two great themes.

One is the splendours and miseries of what it is to be human and mortal; to be one of those 'who have', as Achilles tells Priam, 'sorrow woven in the very pattern of our lives'; 'for whose feet', as Sarpedon on the Trojan side puts it, 'Death has a thousand pitfalls, and no man can save himself or cheat him.' Violent death in all its forms is examined in the *Iliad* in a warrior class for whom, because of the spiritual demands it makes, extinction in battle surpasses every other human experience. This is the warrior ethos.

But not all the characters in the *Iliad* belong to that class. Thousands of 'average and inferior troops' are slaughtered; their deaths go unrecorded, they remain anonymous. There are women too, who are traded like cattle, or worry and grieve, and if they survive are carried off, like Hecuba, Cassandra and Hector's wife Andromache, as spoils of war. 'Heroes' in their dozens *are* named, and their deaths are described in shocking anatomical detail, but fewer than a score of them emerge as living characters: Agamemnon and Meneleus, old Nestor, Achilles and Patroclus, Odysseus, the two Ajaxes and Diomedes among the Greeks, Hector, Paris, Glaucus, Sarpedon, Aeneas among the Trojans. These are 'leaders', and a man who leads, as Odysseus insists, 'is duty bound to stand unflinchingly and to kill or die'. He has chosen war as the context for what Necessity demands of him: a death.

'There were times at home,' Achilles tells the ambassadors who come to tempt him back into battle, 'when I had no higher ambition than to marry some suitable girl of my own class and enjoy the fortune my father Peleus had made . . . But Destiny has left me two courses on my journey to the grave. If I stay here and play my part in the siege of Troy there is no homecoming for me, though I shall win eternal fame. If I go home to my own country, I shall be spared an early death but my name will be lost.'

He chooses fame, of course: but later, in the Afterlife, in his bitter understanding at last of what it is to be alive and living, he tells Odysseus, who visits him there: 'Better to work the soil as a serf, on hire to some impoverished landless peasant, than to be a king among the dead.' But that is in another poem.

The other great theme of the work is what Simone Weil calls 'the greatest calamity the human race can experience', the destruction of that noblest and most complex of man's achievements, that embodiment of co-operation and neighbourliness, of order and art and industry and the law, a city.

Troy, standing at the beginning of all western history – no, before those remote beginnings – is emblematic of every city, in every war, in the twenty-seven centuries since Homer created his epic song of mourning for individual loss and the destruction of many-towered 'holy Ilium'.

Two groups make up the opposing forces here: an army of invading heroes, plus foot soldiers and servants – a loose confederation of opportunistic heroes and their allies – and Troy's beleaguered citizens; highly civilised – perhaps even over-civilised – town-dwellers, luxuriously domesticated, as we see in the description in Book VI of Priam's palace and its extended household of his sons and their wives, and in every way courteous and stylishly refined. Hector speaks of the Trojan ladies in their trailing gowns. Priam, in a bitter moment after Hector has been killed, accuses his remaining sons of being 'no more than heroes of the dance, who win your laurels on the ballroom floor when you are not robbing your own people of their sheep and kids'.

The invaders, rough farmers and family men, are far from home. 'Home' is what the Trojans have to defend. As one of them, Dolon, tells Odysseus and Ajax in a chance night encounter, 'As for our allies, they are asleep. They leave us to keep watch. *Their* women and children are not lying close at hand.'

Hector, who has the heavy responsibility of being the protector of Troy, is the most rounded and sympathetic character in the poem. He has no illusions about what is at stake. We see him in an intimate moment, at home with his wife and child. 'Yet I am not so much distressed,' he tells Andromache, 'by what the Trojans will suffer, or Hecuba, or King Priam, or all my gallant brothers whom the enemy will fling down in the dust, as by the thought of you, dragged off weeping by some man-at-arms to slavery. I see you in Argos, toiling for some other woman at the loom, or carrying water from an alien well, a helpless drudge with no will of your own. "There goes the wife of Hector," they will say when they see you in tears . . . And every time you hear it you will feel another pang at the loss of the one man who might have kept you free.'

He holds his arms out to take the child, Astyanax: 'But the boy shrank back with a cry . . . alarmed by his father's appearance. He was frightened by the bronze of the helmet and the horsehair plume he saw nodding grimly down at him. His father and his lady mother had to laugh.'

The moment, for all its lightness, is charged with pathos. It is also prophetic. Later, just such an armed man will snatch Astyanax from his mother's arms and cast him down from the walls of Troy.

*

Athenian scholars of the fourth century BC, and critics in eighteenth-century Europe who insisted on decorum and the rules, took Homer to task for the inappropriateness to epic dignity of his similes. But for ordinary readers these have always provided some of the *Iliad*'s best-loved passages.

Sharply observed and down-to-earth, these small life-studies establish, amid so much striving and so much angry strife, what the norm might be, and offer a critique, typical of Homer's complex and contradictory view, of the warrior's cult of death. At the most unlikely moments, the poem shifts perspective to take in a world of farming, herding, hunting, the raising of crops and vines; of seafaring and weather-watching; or, more surprisingly, 'an honest woman balancing the wool against the weights to make sure of the meagre pittance she is earning for her children', or 'a little girl trotting at her mother's side and begging to be carried, plucking her skirt and looking up with streaming eyes till at last she takes her in her arms'; or again, 'a boy at the seaside playing childish games with the sand, building a castle to amuse himself, and then, with his hands and feet, destroying the whole work for fun'.

This is like the shield that Hephaestus makes for Achilles in Book XIII, which shows two cities; one beleaguered like Troy by an army, the other the scene of weddings, banquets, wise men sitting in judgement, fields with hired reapers and herds of sheep and cattle, and at last 'a dancing-floor, with youths and marriageable maidens hand in hand, dancing'.

Two visions: of warriors at their business, obsessed with the inevitability of death, and to balance this, the dailyness of life and living.

Two other aspects of the poem have over the

centuries attracted critical complaint. One is Homer's irreverence towards the gods, the other the sometimes unheroic light in which his 'heroes' are seen. Both, to us, seem refreshingly modern.

The Olympian gods, each with a name and a distinct personality, embody those undefinable forces in us, and in the world around us, that govern human existence: earthquakes, storms, such outbreaks of chaos as rebellion and war, but also the full range of sexual proclivities, and madness and psychotic rage. The pantheon on Olympus is a family – we would call it a dysfunctional one – whose antics, as Homer presents them, are all too human in being for the most part absurd.

Father Zeus (a serial philanderer) has supreme authority, but his sister/spouse, Hera, his two brothers, Ares and Poseidon, his children – Aphrodite (fathered by Zeus alone), Athene (Hera's daughter), and Leto's twins, Apollo and Artemis – constantly undermine his will with special pleading, or through plots, or in open rebellion. Entirely self-willed, they take sides in human affairs, intervene on behalf of their favourites, are childishly vindictive; and since they are immortal, and know nothing of human fear or grief, know nothing either of human kindness or compassion.

When Homer calls one of his heroes 'godlike', the compliment has a double edge. It suggests that in being superhuman like the gods he is less than human as well. Hence those occasions when heroes, like the gods, act in ways that are unworthy of them. A lot of the *Iliad* is about men and gods behaving badly.

When a man behaves badly the result is tragic. When gods do so, because it is petty and incongruous, it can also be comic.

Aphrodite is wounded in the hand and flies weeping home. 'Father Zeus,' her sister Athene bitchily observes, 'I hope you will not take it amiss when I suggest your Cyprian daughter must have been at work again, luring Achaean women into the arms of the Trojans she loves so dearly [a sly reference to Paris]'. 'One of these ladies evidently wears a golden brooch, and Aphrodite scratched her dainty hand on it . . .

'This only drew a smile from the Father of men and gods. But he called Aphrodite to his side and said: "Fighting, my child, is not for you. *You* are in charge of wedlock and the tender passions. We will leave the enterprising War-god and Athene to look after military affairs."'

What is so astonishing, always, is the even-handedness with which Homer, unlike the gods, deals with both sides of the conflict. The contrast is with that other great foundation book of our culture, the Hebrew Bible. Its great subject, the redemption of a fallen world, lies beyond the classical mind, but its vision of the damned and the saved allows for nothing of Homer's impartiality and noble compassion. The enemies of its chosen people – Philistines, Canaanites, Medes and Persians – are all equally beneath contempt.

Homer's largeness of spirit shows itself in the great penultimate scene of the poem, when Priam's eyes dwell on the killer of his son and he sees 'with admiration how big and beautiful Achilles was . . . and Achilles noted with equal admiration the noble looks and utterance of Dardanian Priam'. This is the same new-found magnanimity with which the Greeks treat one another at the funeral games for Patroclus.

We glimpse it again in an image, a moment of suspended stillness, that exists for once to illustrate nothing but itself: 'There are nights when the upper air is windless and the stars in heaven stand out in their full splendour round the moon; when every mountain-top and headland and ravine starts into view, as the infinite depths of the sky are torn open to the very firmament . . . There were a thousand fires burning on the plain, and round each one sat fifty men in the light of the blaze, while the horses stood by their chariots, munching white barley and rye.' The lovely inclusiveness of that looks forward to Shakespeare or Tolstoy.

The *Iliad* reminds us that we inhabit a world of unfinished stories, and echoes, the repetition of age-old horrors and miseries. No wonder, in a month when the news is yet again out of Gaza and Ashkelon, that for those, as Simone Weil wrote in 1942, 'who perceive force, today as yesterday, at the centre of human history, the *Iliad* is its most beautiful and purest mirror'.

Australian Literary Review, *2009*

THE ART OF LOVE

THE *ARS AMATORIA* PRESENTS itself as a didactic poem in the manner of Vergil's *Georgics*, but if we expect it to be solemn and improving we will from the start be confounded. Its subject is neither farming nor military tactics, hunting, horsemanship, seafaring, rhetoric or any other practical and socially useful activity. In the topsy-turvy 'modern' world that Ovid introduces us to, the *flaneur*'s world of cruising the streets of a vast cosmopolitan city – of shopping and partygoing; of theatres, taverns, temples, synagogues, colonnades, racetracks, piazzas – his subject is the entirely unsolemn and to this point unconsidered art, or so the poet would have us believe, of getting and keeping a lover.

Highly coloured, allusive, audaciously tongue-in-cheek, the *Ars Amatoria* is from first line to last a series of surprising and provocative reversals, not only of established literary conventions but of anything that even the most alert and knowing reader might expect.

Comic disproportion is its method. Petty concerns are illustrated with large examples, great matters with ones that are trivial. Moral tags are misapplied, old tales introduced on the most tenuous pretext and given new twists, arguments playfully exaggerated until they collapse under their own weight – it is the playfulness not the argument that we are meant to approve and be impressed by; psychological analysis, as in the recounting of Pasiphae's passion for the bull, is pursued to the point where it becomes clearly and comically absurd. Seriousness is at every turn averted, but with so disarming a mixture of slyness and candour, and so much infectious joy in the doing of it, that to charge the poet with crime – lèse-majesté or libertinism or the corruption of youth – would be, to steal an image from a later Augustan, like breaking a butterfly on a wheel. Is this why it took Augustus so long to accuse and punish Ovid?

In AD 8, a good seven years after the poem first made its spectacular appearance, Ovid was banished to Tomis on the Black Sea, a place from which, despite many appeals for clemency, he was never to return. The *Ars Amatoria* is cited as one part of his offence, and it is not difficult to see in the poem what the emperor might have found offensive.

At its centre is a character that was to have a long history in poems of this kind, and not only in Latin – the modern lover; the carefree, pleasure-loving man-about-town who has dropped out of the world of serious civic duty and become a hero not of the battle-field or the law courts but of the bedchamber, where the only 'virtue' he recognises is play. The poem really is subversive – not in the challenge it offers to marriage and the new morality, or because it has the effrontery to claim for the lover the same 'professional' status as the farmer, the soldier, the holder of high public office, but because it makes the role it creates so invitingly attractive; most of all, because it establishes the lover/ poet as the emperor of an alternative and privately constituted state. As John Donne, one of Ovid's later incarnations, puts it, 'She is all States, and all Princes, I / Nothing else is.' The poem's ostensible subject, the art of love, is a decoy. The real subject is the poet himself. To be a *poet* – to be *the* poet, Ovid – is to be a world unto yourself. The emperor's world, the great world of Rome, is simply his scene of operations; at the most, 'material', to be treated as he will. That is the immodest claim. No wonder Augustus felt he needed to act.

Around this lively and youthfully impulsive *persona* (the poet himself, we might note, was in his middle forties) Ovid organises a spectacular ado, a series of brilliant sideshows in which what is on display is the poet's delight in his own talent; the range of his erudition, his verbal dexterity and wit, his inventiveness in painting scenes of sweeping grandeur but also, since he has what we would now call a cinematic eye, zooming in on illuminating close-ups. The poet can take literally anything into his poem in the assurance that what will hold it together is his own mercurial presence, as guide, confidant, provocateur, storyteller, picture maker, mock scholar, mock sage, magician, stage manager.

At one moment he is leading us on a conducted tour of the city's sights and monuments – with time out to comment on the usefulness of each as a pick-up place; in the next he is playing knucklebones or spillikins, or recommending hairstyles or footwear or health resorts, or diverting us with old tales retold. Of Pasiphae and her bull, of the birdman Daedalus, of Mars and Venus, Cephalus and Procris; throwing out hints along the way to a whole company of poets and playwrights and novelists to come.

To the school of English poets we call Metaphysical, for example, who will find in his unexpected juxtapositions, his yoking together of disparate worlds and objects, the way to a new kind of imagery. To Molière for *Les précieuses ridicules* and *Les femmes savantes*. To a long line of eighteenth-century epistolary novelists. Even, perhaps, in his proposal that the safest way of transmitting a message is to write it on the back of the messenger, to a twentieth-century filmmaker, Peter Greenaway, for *The Pillow Book*.

It is the protean inclusiveness of the *Ars Amatoria*, its joy in the variousness and contrariety of things, their lovely capacity for surprise and paradox, that has made it such a treasure-house of literary tropes and genres, such a gallery of pictures that need only the stroke of a brush to make them actual paintings. Titian, Rubens, Poussin and others had only to turn to the verbal pictures here – Bacchus in a chariot drawn by tigers, a drunken Silenus falling sideways off his ass, Cephalus stretched out in a grassy clearing – to discover the program, down to the smallest detail, for some of the greatest paintings of the Renaissance and Baroque.

One of Ovid's most sympathetic qualities for those who came later was his own sense of Lateness – of being, as he must have seen it, post-classical. But what he also demonstrated, and by brilliant example, was that all we need to make old material new is freshness of invention and a previously unconsidered point of view.

Walking along the shore with Calypso, Ulysses maps the Trojan plain for her by drawing with a stick in the sand, and so Ovid embarks, once again, on the well-known story. But Ulysses has barely got started on his 'epic' when a wave sweeps up the beach, and in a wonderfully dramatic and affecting image Troy and all the old world of gods and heroes is once more obliterated.

In the retelling of the Daedalus story, one of the most extended and fully imagined in the poem, an aerial view of the Greek islands Naxos, Paros and Delos – in itself a remarkable piece of image-making – is momentarily suspended while Ovid shows us his two birdmen from another angle; through the eyes now of a supernumerary angler on the beach below. More than fifteen centuries later, Brueghel would appropriate this extraordinary image for a famous painting, and four centuries later again, W. H. Auden will use it in an equally famous poem.

The *Ars Armatoria*, mock serious as it is and focused only on the immediate and personal, has turned out, by a kind of miracle, to be timeless.

To the wandering scholars of the twelfth and thirteenth centuries, as to the authors of *The Romance of the Rose* and Chaucer in the fourteenth, Ovid seemed like a man of 'modern' sensibility, a contemporary out of his time; and he appeared that way also to the poets of the Renaissance. His dedication to what the Elizabethan poet George Chapman called 'Ovid's banquet of sense' made him a natural alternative to the idealism of Petrarch and the Petrarchans. It was his unashamed joy in carnality, and in sensory phenomena of every sort, that led the seventeen-year-old Marlowe to translate the *Amores* while he was still at Cambridge, and for Frances Meres, writing in 1585, Shakespeare was the 'sweet witty soul' of Ovid mellifluously reborn, as in France it is what a rejuvenated Ronsard turned to in the second and third book of his *Amours*. When Goethe, in the fifth of his *Roman Elegies*, taps out his hexameters on the back of a sleeping girl, it is surely Ovid who is there in the shadows behind him, as it must have been Ovid, as much as any of the Italian painters, or Winckelmann with his promise of 'classical ground', that drew the great northerner into that area of his nature he called Italy.

Ovid represents the playful, lightly irreverent element in our culture that once a place has been found for it we cannot do without. We have only to catch the echo of his voice in our own language, as we do in Sir Thomas Wyatt or the early Donne, or Sir John Suckling or Frank O'Hara, to recognise a lost but living contemporary whose boldness is a challenge to our own, and the charm of whose companionship remains, as it has always been, irresistible.

Introduction to The Art of Love, *translated by James Michie, Modern Library Classics, 2002*

RELATIVE FREEDOM

THE TEMPEST IS A SPECIAL case among Shakespeare's plays. The editors of the First Folio, as long ago as 1623, chose it to introduce their complete edition of the Works, and as the final statement of our greatest writer playgoers have long felt that it ought to have some special significance, some special message even; it ought to be a summing-up, a gesture of farewell. Then too, it's a play that is full of mysterious happenings; a fairytale with a shipwreck, an enchanted island, a magician with godlike powers, a prince who has to win the magician's daughter by undergoing an ordeal and submitting to a test of chastity. Surely with all these properties of the folk-tale, the dream-play, it is also some sort of allegory, and it has, of course, especially in the past half-century, become a source-book for symbol-hunters and dream-mongers of every sort: Freudians, Jungians, Neo-Platonists, pullers of the Great Chain of Being. Prospero's island, as he himself puts it, has certain 'subtleties'. One of them is to appear in a quite different form to each person who looks at it. To Gonzalo it is green, to Alonso tawny, and for the most part what men see in it is a reflection of themselves.

Of course I don't mean by this that *The Tempest* has *no* meaning, or that we are to take it as mere whimsy, a sort of Jacobean *Peter Pan*. In fact another difficulty of the play is that it is so full of ideas that matter – questions that were just beginning to be asked in Shakespeare's day and that we have been puzzling over ever since. Questions about the true nature of man, for example. Is he in essence innocent or inevitably fallen and corrupt, though redeemable either by education or through divine grace? Questions about the need for authority and order – we might remember here those extraordinary proto-Communist agitators of the early seventeenth century, the Diggers and Levellers, who with a simple rhyme, 'When Adam delved and Eve span / Who was then the gentleman?' challenged authority, hierarchy and property, all three. Questions about Europe's relationship to the New World, whose discovery had upset so many comfortable notions about man and his place in the universe, and raised new problems about civilised man's rights over, and responsibilities towards, the inhabitants of the new lands – a subject we would now call 'colonialism'.

But first and foremost we need to remember that *The Tempest* is a comedy, perhaps the most sophisticated Shakespeare ever wrote. And since Shakespeare is, among other things, our greatest comic dramatist, that is to put the play in a very high category indeed.

Or is it? Can a comedy really be great literature? As great, say, as *Oedipus* or *Hamlet* or *King Lear*? And what *is* comedy anyway?

Let me say right away that comedy seems to me to be the greatest of all forms of drama, and comedy of a serious kind – comedy that doesn't just fall about or send things up, but tries to make a full statement about life and its possibilities, that sort of comedy – is also the most difficult sort of drama to write.

What tragedy presents us with is what we know is true but cannot bear to live with – the facts of what it is to be human: that death is inevitable; that outrageous accidents and muddles upset the best laid plans of men; that time is the destroyer of all things; that fate or the gods are more powerful than the wisest and best of us. Tragedy explores what it means to be subject to the contradictions of existence. It pushes out towards the limits of human necessity to discover that there is no escape: once a choice has been made it cannot be reversed; every event has its inevitable consequence; the clock goes on ticking. Great tragedies like *Oedipus* or *Macbeth*, great tragic moments like the end of Faustus, have for us the fascination of a nightmare – someone else's nightmare. The world closes in around us. We are trapped by our very nature as men. But comedy somehow – and this is the point I want to make about it – opens the trap and sets us free again. The world of comedy is one in which we are not ruled by necessity after all. Some other quite miraculous force is at work within it to sort out the muddles, to restore lost daughters and wives, to wipe out old terrors, rectify misunderstandings, sometimes even to raise the dead and prove that old crimes were never really committed. All the possibilities are opened again and we get what we never get in real life, a chance to begin our lives over again. And this happens not because it is the way things are but because the comic dramatist makes it so. Comedy is an act of faith about the way things might be rather than a picture of how they are. To write a play like *The Tempest* you have to believe something, and the play is so liberating to us because it is itself a marvellous act of freedom on the part of the man who made it.

So without pinning the play down to one of those schemes that critics are so fond of, in which Prospero equals the imagination, or the intellect or God, and Caliban, Ariel and the rest are dislocated bits and pieces of his psyche, I would like to suggest that *The Tempest* raises questions about our human limitations and possibilities that we might want, in the end, to call religious, and takes them back into the realm of politics and the ordinary affairs of daily living. Shakespeare's play is a medium in which questions about freedom, responsibility, order, authority, compassion, forgiveness, self-knowledge – grace, even – are free to raise themselves and be acted out in the very fabric of the play; but they are acted out, not argued over, and almost never resolved.

The key notion, perhaps, is the one we have already pointed to in talking about the total effect of the play itself: the notion of freedom. It presents itself in many different forms.

There is, for example, Prospero's freedom through his art to control nature and – in the last resort – the lives of the other characters in the play. It is, we might think, a freedom that is rather like the freedom of the artist himself, who also has control of the plot of his play and over the characters within it. But we must beware of equating the two. There are areas of the play that Shakespeare is aware of and Prospero is not, and areas also that lie outside Prospero's control. Antonio, for example, remains free at the end of the play not to repent, not to join the happy circle of the redeemed. And there is the whole question of Ariel's lack of freedom, his bondage to Prospero, and Caliban's lack of freedom, his slavery. Both of these, it seems to me, raise questions about the sort of authority Prospero exercises in the play that ought to prevent our accepting too completely the notion that Shakespeare and Prospero speak as one.

That question of Caliban's slavery, for example. Is it, as some commentators suggest, simply a 'natural' aspect of Caliban's role as 'salvage man'? Isn't there something in his great denunciation of Prospero in I, ii that challenges, in its very tone, the idea that civilised man's rights over the savage are natural and absolute?

> This island's mine, by Sycorax my mother,
> Which thou tak'st from me. When thou cam'st first
> Thou strok'st me, and made much of me; wouldst
>   give me
> Water with berries in't; and teach me how
> To name the bigger light, and how the less,
> That burn by day and night; and then I lov'd thee
> And show'd thee all the qualities o' th' isle,
> The fresh springs, brine pits, barren place and fertile:
> Curs'd be I that did so! All the charms
> Of Sycorax, toads, beetles, bats, light on you!
> For I am all the subjects that you have,
> Which first was mine own King: and here you sty me
> In this hard rock, while you do keep from me
> The rest o' th' isle.
>
> I ii 333–346

Caliban is allowed to state his case and it stands – even after we have discovered that he has tried to rape Miranda and people the island with Calibans.

Real questions are being raised here about the nature of Prospero's authority and the reasons for Caliban's loss of freedom that are connected with the whole political and moral world of the play. And a great deal of the play is concerned with questions of politics: Prospero's abjuration of his political responsibilities at Milan; the acts of usurpation there, and Sebastian's attempted act of usurpation on the island; the attempted usurpation of Stephano. And a great deal of the play is also concerned, as a corollary, with the ways in which men either retain their freedom or relinquish it to the will of others. We see Caliban fall into the trap of making himself the slave of a new master to be rid of the old – and a worse master at that. We see Ferdinand put in much the same position as Caliban when he is set, like Caliban, to drawing logs. But his attitude is very different:

> I am, in my condition,
> A prince, Miranda: I do think, a King;
> I would not so! – and would no more endure
> This wooden slavery than to suffer
> The flesh-fly blow my mouth. Hear my soul speak:
> The very instant that I saw you, did
> My heart fly to your service; there resides,
> To make me slave to it; and for your sake
> I am this patient log-man.

III i 59–67

At his very first meeting with Miranda, in lines that must immediately link him with both Caliban and Ariel, he discovers a new kind of freedom in the idea of bondage itself:

> Might I but through my prison once a day
> Behold this maid: all corners else o' the earth
> Let liberty make use of; space enough
> Have I in such a prison.

I ii 493–6

Ferdinand's attitude to bondage is very different from the others' – and Shakespeare shows it as just that, different, another way of looking at a complex question, but not an attitude that necessarily 'places' the other attitudes and demands our unqualified assent; any more than Prospero's right to power is given our unqualified assent. Ferdinand's attitude leaves the questions raised by Caliban and Ariel unanswered.

One of the claims one would want to make for *The Tempest*, and for Shakespeare, is this peculiar capacity for letting every side of a question speak for itself; for presenting every side as part of a multi-faceted view. We should be very careful indeed before we dismiss any argument that the play allows to be expressed, and before we accept any speech from any character, even Prospero, as 'trumping' another character or his point of view.

Take Gonzalo's speech about his commonwealth in II i. We know that it is taken, almost word for word, from Montaigne, and Shakespeare's more hard-headed attitudes, and the context of the play itself, would seem to refute Gonzalo's breathless idealism. But is that really so? Here is Gonzalo's vision of the just society, the good life:

> . . . no kind of traffic
> Would I admit: no name of magistrate;
> Letters should not be known; riches, poverty
> And use of service, none; contract, succession
> Bourn, bound of land, tilth, vineyard, none;
> No use of metal, corn, or wine, or oil;
> No occupation; all men idle, all;
> And women too, but innocent and pure: . . .
> All things in common Nature should produce
> Without sweat or endeavour: treason, felony,
> Sword, pike, knife, gun or need of any engine,
> Would I not have; but Nature should bring forth,
> Of its own kind, all foison, all abundance
> To feed my innocent people.
>
> II i 144–160

It is, of course, a marvellously attractive picture, and one that has haunted men as a possibility, as an alternative, from Vergil's *Fourth Eclogue* about the return of the Golden Age, through the Levellers and early

Communists down to our own hippy communes. No commercialism, no class distinctions, no use of other people's labour – you will see how that is connected with the last idea we were looking at and Prospero's rights over Caliban and Ariel. No inherited wealth. All property in common, no monopolies over the essentials of life; no violence, no politicking, every man free to do his own thing. It's a marvellous dream and it needs to be stated here against the whole world of imposed order and authority that is another aspect of the play's action. Like Caliban's denunciation of Prospero it stands. It is not 'placed' by the mean interjections of Antonio and Sebastian or by Gonzalo's failure to locate Tunis and his rather prissy euphemism about 'widow Dido'. What does question it is Gonzalo's own admission that it will exist only if people are all 'innocent' and 'pure'. And as the little community on the island itself shows, this is, regrettably, not so. He is barely finished speaking before treachery, violence and ambition for ascendancy are revealed in the scene Shakespeare contrives between Sebastian and Antonio, and of course the point is made elsewhere when we see Stephano, in a low parody of the two courtiers, setting up as ruler over his fellow servant.

The question that is being raised here is why the state and all its paraphernalia of authority might be necessary – but also how it comes into existence, and through all this, Gonzalo's vision stands as an alternative. The political point turns on the moral question of man's nature and the limitations it might put upon his possibilities. Antonio and Sebastian can be cynical about these possibilities, but Shakespeare, one wants to assert, is not. Only hard-headedly realistic, and he lets the cynical view be stated to show the difference.

Shakespeare asks us to observe man, in his play, not without idealism but without illusions. Man is man. There are no gods among us, though the naïve are always eager to find one (that is, a superior being they can adore). Caliban makes that mistake with Stephano, though he does at last come to realise it:

What a thrice-double ass
Was I, to take this drunkard for a god,
And worship this dull fool!

V i 295–7

But Ferdinand does much the same thing with Miranda:

Most sure the goddess
On whom these airs attend! Vouchsafe my prayer
May know if you remain upon this island;

I ii 424–6

And one of the most moving things in the play is his reassessment of all this, and his real discovery of her, when, in Act V, to his father's question:

> Is she the goddess that hath sever'd us
> And brought us thus together?
>
> V i 188–9

Ferdinand replies:

> Sir, she is mortal;
> But by immortal Providence she's mine.
>
> V i 188–9

Miranda has in the same way taken Ferdinand for something more than human:

> I might call him
> A thing divine; for nothing natural
> I ever saw so noble.
>
> I ii 420–2

And when Prospero, in a strange echo of Caliban's accusation to him, accuses Ferdinand of having come to usurp the isle, Ferdinand's denial: 'No, as I am a man!', and Miranda's 'There's nothing ill can dwell in such a temple', immediately raises the question that is to be put most clearly in Act V, the question we have already discovered in Gonzalo's common-wealth speech and which the play comes back to at every point. Just what is man? How can we reconcile the presence of evil in him with the presence of nobility?

> O wonder!
> How many goodly creatures are there here!
> How beauteous mankind is! O brave new world,
> That has such people in't.
>
> V i 181–4

Miranda is of course facing a mixed bag of humanity that includes the men who drove her father out and tried to kill them both, as well as the old councillor whose compassion and charity saved them, and the usual timeserving courtiers who blow with the wind – a not unrepresentative group of us all, we might think. Her affirmation of faith in mankind is only partly modified by 'dramatic irony'. Prospero's 'Tis new to thee' points to her lack of experience, but it alerts us as well to his own weary disillusion. Her affirmation stands. And the phrase she chooses, 'O brave new world', looks in two opposite directions in a marvellous and typically Shakespearean way.

To Miranda that 'brave new world' is the ordinary world we all know. It is us and Shakespeare's contemporary audience. But to them it must also have suggested the New World of the Americas, the lands beyond the sea and the miraculous presence of people out there beyond the known world whose existence was to them what the discovery of men on other planets would be to us. What were the men of the New World like? Were they innocent unfallen Adams or men like other men? That is one of the questions the play takes up through the character of Caliban, who is surely the most interesting and original creation of the play, the character who makes the largest demands on Shakespeare's imagination and on ours.

It is easy to simplify what Shakespeare has actually presented in him. Critics often ask us to see the play as a grouping of characters round this central figure of the savage, and it is useful to take up the contrasts Shakespeare has provided – and sometimes the comparisons – between, say, Caliban and Miranda, Caliban and Ferdinand, Caliban and the degenerate nobles, Caliban and the other characters here who stand outside the charmed circle of privilege and birth, the lowlife Trinculo and Stephano.

These contrasts are illuminating, and our judgement of Caliban changes with each of them – and our ideas of the other characters also change as we judge *them* against *him*. But that is not in the last resort what Caliban is there for. He has a life of his own in the play that is larger, and richer and more complex and challenging to us, than any part he might play in a formal scheme. Most of all we should not impose on him any role as 'salvage man' whose attributes we can adduce from elsewhere. If we know anything at all about Shakespeare it is that he is never dependent on conventional types or conventional attitudes. His Caliban is about as likely to resemble the stock savage as Shylock, for example, resembles the stock Jew.

That Shakespeare was interested in the people of the new world we know from the play itself. Textual evidence shows that he had been reading Montaigne's essay 'On Cannibals' and Trinculo refers to contemporary curiosity about Indians in general: 'There' (he means in England) 'when they will not give a doit to relieve a lame beggar they will lay out ten to see a dead Indian'. Shakespeare is teasing as well as amusing his audience when he introduces into his play a live Indian and then asks them to make a challenging reassessment of both Indians and themselves.

That suggests one way in which Caliban might question accepted notions of where Indians stand in the scheme of things. What about some of the other characteristics that are usually attributed to him? Let us admit that Caliban is surly, that he harbours murderous grudges against Prospero:

Why, as I told thee, tis a custom with him
I' the afternoon to sleep: there thou mayst brain him,

Having first seized on his books; or with a log
Batter his skull, or paunch him with a stake
Or cut his wezand with a knife.

III ii 85–89

The brutality is obvious enough. No attempt is made to conceal or sentimentalise Caliban's savagery – though it is in no way worse, we might think, than the civilised brutality of Sebastian and Antonio, and might even be more excusable; Caliban has been genuinely wronged. But what about some of the qualities that are supposed to flow from this: Caliban's inability for example to function on any but the lowest level of sensuality and lust. What are we to make of these lines that come in the same speech as the lines I have just quoted?

And that most deeply to consider is
The beauty of his daughter; he himself
Calls her a nonpareil: I never saw a woman
But only Sycorax my dam and she;
And she as far surpasseth Sycorax
As great'st does least.

III ii 96–101

Now Shakespeare is most careful there. The word 'nonpareil' is attributed to Prospero, and Caliban takes it up in his admission that he has no grounds for comparison except the rather comic one, we might think, of Miranda and Sycorax. But isn't there a real capacity for wonder in these lines that relates them immediately to the wonder of Ferdinand, and to Miranda herself when she encounters Ferdinand? Her only comparison was with her father and Caliban.

It isn't simply that a contrast is being established here that 'places' Caliban. Rather a series of comparisons is set up that relates all three, and shows them, within their different world selves, as alike. If anything, it establishes Caliban as a figure of real pathos. And this is not entirely destroyed when, with a reference back to his own ambitions, he brings Stephano into the field of view with:

> Ay, lord; she will become thy bed, I warrant,
> And bring thee forth brave brood.
>
> III ii 102–3

Caliban's responses veer sharply from what is fine to what is utterly crude, but what we need to have an ear for is the shift.

His capacity to respond to the island's music, for example, isn't simply a reference to music's capacity to 'appeal to the beast that lacks reason', as Frank Kermode would have us believe. It is the source for Caliban of a deeply felt vision of other possibilities, of an existence he has glimpsed but not yet fully comprehended:

And sometimes voices
That, if I then had waked after long sleep,
Will make me sleep again; and then, in dreaming,
The clouds methought would ope and show riches
Ready to drop on me; that when I wak'd
I cried to dream again.

III ii 136–141

Shakespeare allows Caliban access here to the full range of the play's poetry, and it is surely no accident that the 'clouds', the 'show', the 'sleep' of his vision recur in Prospero's famous speech in Act IV.

And Caliban's response to the island's music makes a further point. It is the sense in which the island exists for him – and through him for *us* – as it does for no-one else in the play.

Prospero of course has power over the island, the power of magic – white magic – attained through the highest exercise of the intellect. But Caliban's possession derives from power of another sort altogether. He has mapped it all with his senses. It is his in a way that Prospero could barely conceive of, though Shakespeare does. Look again at Caliban's denunciation in Act I, with its evocation of 'all the qualities o' th' isle/The fresh springs, brine-pits, barren place and fertile', or the speech in Act III where, like the gullible and pathetically generous natives of so many unfortunate isles, he offers to share his gifts with the white colonist Stephano:

I'll show thee the best springs, I'll pluck thee
    berries . . .
I prithee let me bring thee where crabs grow
And I with my long nails will dig thee pignuts;
Show thee a jay's nest, and instruct thee how
To snare the nimble marmoset; I'll bring thee
To clustering filberts, and sometimes I'll get thee
Young scammels from the rock.

II ii 160 . . . 166–72

It is only through Caliban that we get this sense of the richness of the island, its tumbling fecundity. His capacity to name things, and by naming evoke them, is a different sort of magic from Prospero's but no less powerful and real. It might remind us of the extraordinary way our own indigenous people possess the land, through folk stories, taboos, song cycles, and have made it part of the very fabric of their living; or to leap elsewhere, we might think of Lévi-Strauss' discovery that the way native people build up and preserve in their memory a knowledge of their environment is every bit as true, and scientific and useful, as our own. This Shakespeare seems to have discovered intuitively, through Caliban, and it not only challenges Prospero and his magic but questions the sort of assertions Prospero is making when he calls Caliban one 'on whose nature / Nurture can never stick'.

Caliban learns from experience what Prospero can never teach him from books. When he announces at the end of the play, 'I'll be wise hereafter / And seek for grace,' he is surely a character in process of discovering himself and his humanity. He is to be linked equally with all those others for whom Gonzalo speaks in his great summing-up of the play's many discoveries:

and all of us ourselves
When no man was his own

V i 212–13

The questions are radical ones: radical in that they challenge some of our most deeply rooted notions about the play. Prospero's centrality, it seems to me, has never been seriously challenged, and of course once we begin to question it, once we admit that Shakespeare may be questioning it, our whole assumption about the rightness of Prospero's authority and the order he establishes is also in question – and with it most traditional readings of the play. Can we do this without doing violence to what Shakespeare intended?

It has always surprised me that critics have been so willing to accept Prospero as the one and only central consciousness of the play. To do so is to put *The Tempest* in a unique category.

One of the great tests that is put upon us by a Shakespeare play is the test of our capacity to let the play *happen*; to allow different aspects of the play's world to reveal themselves, and challenge or modify one another, without our demanding a simple or single point of view. It is a passion for simplifying, for choosing one view at the expense of all others, that has bedevilled criticism of some of our greatest and most complex plays: *Julius Caesar*, the two parts of *Henry IV*, *Antony and Cleopatra*, *Hamlet*.

The history plays offer us the clearest and most complex view of Shakespeare's attitude to authority, order and the necessity of the law, and none better than the two *Henry IV* plays, whose action ranges from the court to the half-criminal lowlife of Eastcheap, but also takes in the small-town affairs of rural Gloucestershire. Essential to all this are the antics of that Lord of Misrule, the fat knight Falstaff. Shakespeare endows Falstaff with so much wit, so much life, that like Prince Hal we are immediately seduced; how could we fail to be charmed by a figure who creates around himself so much energy, so much delight in play; who stands in such contrast to the cold world of policy, and the institutionalised violence that, in the name of 'honour', creates his own kind of havoc to sustain it? Falstaff's minor forms of criminality, we might think, are a more excusable, because personal and human form of disorder, than the large-scale rebellion of the nobles here, or the act of usurpation that has set Henry on his throne, and the spurious arguments, another kind of untruth, that are brought forward to justify them. Falstaff speaks up for life and for the little man who cannot afford to be more than sometimes virtuous. But then there is that moment on the battlefield, where, after his very amusing rejection of 'Honour', he violates in the most shameful way the body of Hotspur and claims the 'honour' of having killed him. The truth is that however deeply Falstaff engages our sympathy as a loveable rogue, he is also a liar, a coward, and his treatment of Hotspur's body is in every way inexcusable. His rejection then, at the end of the play, is, for an engaged and sympathetic audience, one of the most uncomfortable moments Shakespeare ever created – and it is the measure of his integrity that he does nothing to disguise the fact or make it easier. 'Banish Plump Jack and banish the world' is Falstaff's justification of himself, and it stands. But Prince Hal's earlier fierce assertion, 'I do, I will,' and his cold repetition of it now, 'I know thee not, old man' – as cruel and unacceptable a speech as we get in the plays from even the coldest ruler – also stands. This is Prince Hal acting as he must, like an upholder of order, a lord of rule. Law and order is all we have as a wall against what we are as humans: against criminal self-will, both of the political kind that expresses itself as ambition, oppression, rebellion, usurpation, and the more ordinary crimes of theft, bribery, exploitation practised by a Falstaff.

There is no way out of this dilemma. Shakespeare speaks for both sides, and offers no happy resolution, but we miss the point badly if we see the banishment of Falstaff as Shakespeare's acceptance of the rightness of authority. The regrettable necessity, perhaps. Rightness is another thing altogether.

The question of order and disorder, of the need for authority, is as alive in *The Tempest* as in any of the chronicle plays. There is no reason why Shakespeare should be more willing to accept authority at this point than ten years before – and no reason why he should be more willing to dismiss Caliban's claims against it, and his claim to life, than Falstaff's. Prospero seems to me to share with other such authority figures a quality that makes him not quite human enough – though Shakespeare makes him as human as he can be made.

And the difficulty is not resolved, here or anywhere else. Not resolved because for Shakespeare to remain truthful to the facts, about society, about man, it cannot be resolved. What we get instead are questions that go unanswered on the level of real life while the part of our mind that demands resolution is satisfied by the *shape* of the comedy itself.

The Tempest is a hard-headed and realistic picture of what man is and all that he aspires to. It is also a piece of magic – a fantasy world that reflects our world and its problems but is free, in a way the real world never can be, to find its own conclusion. Here drowned men reappear with not a hair of their head hurt; lost fathers and sons are reunited; lovers discover one another without misunderstanding; old crimes are forgiven and redeemed; tables appear and disappear to music; the gods come down to bless a purely mortal union; Ariel works his way to freedom, Caliban gets his island back.

And at the end, all these characters who have strayed from the way go back to Naples or Milan to live out day by day, in the ordinary world, what they have discovered on their magic island; as we, surely, are asked to translate what Shakespeare has revealed to us in the free world of comedy into the conditional world of the here and now. It is no accident that what carries the characters in *The Tempest* back to their real world is supplied by us. We too have our part in the play.

Admitting as we do that what we have been watching is a play we are invited to step across the gap between illusion and reality and create, with the clapping of our hands, the breeze that will fill the ship's sails and drive Prospero and the others home. Our hands, as Prospero tells us, must set them free.

Free. It comes to us as the last word of all. And what a lovely conceit it is that we are invited to act out as our applause ends the performance and breaks its spell, bringing the inhabitants of this enchanted world back to our own unfree world, that has been trans-figured, while the spell lasts, by a marvellous vision of what it means to exist for a time in a state of more than human possibility.

Address for the English Association,
Sydney University, May 1973

'AUTHOR, AUTHOR!'

I SOMETIMES AMUSE MYSELF by imagining a balmy night, somewhere in the eternal afterlife, when at the end of an ideal performance of *A Midsummer Night's Dream*, say, or *Hamlet*, or *Romeo and Juliet*, the audience springs spontaneously to its feet shouting 'Author, author!', and what follows is an unseemly scramble as the usual contenders make a rush for the stage. I also imagine our man from Stratford remaining quietly in his place; enjoying, with a smile, something he has always had an eye for, the excesses of human folly, but feeling no push, this late in the piece, to jump in and stake his claim.

With half a dozen books on the market in which every fugitive appearance of the name Shakespeare or Shakspere or Shaxpere in the world of documents has been uncovered and explored, the claimants keep coming. Last year a Neville, this year a woman,

'Sidney's sister, Pembroke's mother', Mary Countess of Pembroke, thrust forward now to join Bacon, Marlowe, the Earl of Oxford and the Earl of Derby, all of whom it might seem have better credentials than Will Shakespeare, Gent., the grammar-school boy of Stratford, to be the creator of the forty or so plays we are familiar with, but also, as Dryden called him, 'the largest and most comprehensive soul among all Modern and perhaps Ancient poets'.

The stumbling-block, for those who find one here, is how such a very common person, the son of a minor official in a small country town, a glovemaker and sometime illegal speculator in wool, could acquire the experience – of the court and its manners, the law, the life of a soldier in the field, of foreign places – that would allow him to produce such a body of work, and, considering the limits of his education, to call on allusions from such a range of contemporary and classical culture.

It is easy for scholars who are themselves the products of a good formal education to exaggerate just how much schooling a writer, even a superlatively great one, might need. Easy as well to be misled about the kind of education a writer can best make use of. Henry James, who knew something about writers and the way they work, has this to say in a famous passage from 'The Art of Fiction'. After accepting the commonplace assertion that a writer should write out of his experience, he asks: 'What kind of experience is intended, and where does it begin and end?' He is particularly interested in what might appear to be unlikely cases, the writer who has a grasp of experiences he – or especially she – might seem to have no opportunity for acquiring. 'The young lady living in a village,' he offers as his extreme case, 'has only to be a damsel on whom nothing is lost to make it quite unfair (as it seems to me) to declare to her that she shall have nothing to say of the military'; and he goes on to state the general principle that we might apply to our man:

> The power to guess the unseen from the seen, to trace the implication of things, to judge the whole piece by the pattern, the condition of feeling life in general so completely that you are well on your way to knowing any particular corner of it – this cluster of gifts may almost be said to constitute experience, and they occur in country and in town and in the most differing stages of education.

James' conclusion is that what really matters is that the writer should be one of those 'on whom nothing is lost': that is, an observer, a listener, a close attendant on the world's smallest affairs, a scavenger, a snapper-up of otherwise unconsidered trifles; and that everything he sees, and hears and overhears, should be laid down in his memory, taken into the spider-web of the consciousness and kept there to await the moment when, transformed by imagination, it finds its use.

＊

With almost 150 years of general literacy behind us, it is hard to imagine a time when everything we might need to get hold of in the way of know-how was acquired not through books and reading but through listening, and learned not in the classroom but on the job; when all our beliefs and views were picked up at our parent's knee, or at mealtimes, or through gossip, rumour, hearsay, or from long Sunday sermons at church, or from town-criers or street ballads.

One must have learned very early to be a keen listener, and to be more skilled than we are at holding meaning in suspension to the end of a complex sentence; more alert as well to double meanings and word play, especially when the fine line of meaning might also be a line between beliefs – affiliations – that could get you into serious trouble with the authorities, whose spies were also skilled at eaves-dropping and interpreting, and were everywhere. All this is what the complex syntax of Elizabethan sermons suggests, but also the language of the public theatre, even if we allow for different levels of skill in the listener that would require preachers, and playwrights, to provide different levels of meaning in what they had to say: a general one, easily caught, and a little lower layer, more challenging or subversive, for the discerning.

The point I mean to make is that in an age when some 90 per cent of women and 75 per cent of men were still illiterate, coming to your experience orally, or by direct observation, must still have been the prevailing method, even for those who could read.

A Shakespeare for instance; growing up in a household that was in close contact with such trades as leatherworking, tanning, dyeing, along with other small-town industries such as weaving, brewing, pottery-making, joinery, tiling, thatching, and also, because of his father's dabbling in the wool-trade, with shearing, drenching, dagging, and all the seasonal activities, but all the gossip as well, of such small out-lying communities as Snittersfield, Shottery and the 'pelting farms' beyond.

Village life anywhere is slow, but offers its own absorbing spectacles: recruitment for the various wars, assizes, civic processions and other ceremonies, village games, the visits of travelling players, and all the customs associated with such seasonal festivities as Yuletide, Easter, spring planting and harvest. Rich material for anyone who might have a use for it.

As for the use to which the young Shakespeare put it – we have a very lively picture of what *that* was when we consider Sir Philip Sidney's attack on the English stage in his *Apologie* of c. 1580.

Standing, as he puts it, 'on the authority of the Romans, and before them the Greeks', Sidney mocks the native drama for its crude mixing of the genres – of 'hornpipes and funerals'; for its naivety, its preference, in comedy, for a 'scurrility unworthy of chaste ears' – all deficiencies that make it impossible for a man of his sort to take it seriously.

As for its plots and conventions:

> Now we shall have three ladies walk to gather flowers, and then we must believe the stage is a garden. By and by we hear news of a shipwreck in the same place, and then we are to blame as we accept it not for a rock . . . Two young princes fall in love; after many traverses she is got with child, delivered of a fair boy, he is lost, groweth a man, falleth in love, and is ready to get another child – and all this in two hours space.

Sidney is not a pedant, or not quite. But limited by his higher education, the fineness of his sensibility, his seriousness, and also perhaps his class, he sees in this popular entertainment only what is low and uncultivated, and in the readiness of its audience to go along with it only an ignorant willingness to be entertained at any price.

But suppose he had been less ready to defer to

classical authority. Mightn't he have seen something different? An original and entirely *English* form of playmaking, with a preference for modes that were mixed rather than pure and could be played off one against the other to provide contrast. A form based, in a very Anglo-Saxon way, on practice – what can be made to *work* – rather than the application of principle. Mightn't he have been led to praise the form for its openness, its capacity to let richness in? Mightn't he have found praise, as well, for the responsiveness of its audience? To surprise, wonder, variety of tone and effect?

All this is what the young Shakespeare found himself happily working with – and I say 'found himself' because he must simply have set himself to work at first with what he was given: an eclectic mix of traditional and folk material, of slapstick, Senecan horror, Italian or Spanish romance, for an audience that was prepared to be transported wherever the play might take them; with an ear for language that was elevating and rich, but a taste as well for the scurrilous that was almost the equal of Shakespeare's own. With no qualms, or so it appears, about the purely commercial nature of what he was engaged in, the young Shakespeare simply set himself to do as good a job as his talent, his interest, his experience allowed him to do.

Like his great Spanish contemporary, Lope de Vega, he made a distinction between his poems, which *do* aim to be literature, and the plays, which do not. He does not lack 'immortal longings', and in the sonnets makes his own high claim: 'So long as man can breathe or eyes can see / So long live this, and this gives life to thee.' He was proud of the sonnets, and passed them round, as gentlemen did, 'among his friends'; he even allowed them to be published. The plays were something else. Not Works, but work. If he worked on them to the top of his bent it was because he was by temperament the complete professional and could do no less. But what they belonged to was not literature but the lively and engaging world of entertainment: in a continuum with such other forms of popular diversion as bull-baiting, bear-baiting, cock-fighting, and in its darker aspects, the spectacle provided by exhibitionary torments and executions, the state's own theatre of cruelty and last words. Anything he hit upon and drew out of himself, in the way of originality and daring, must have emerged in the heat of the work itself, as his talent and interest, both of which as it happens were prodigious, discovered possibilities in the material before him that till he conceived of them, 'in the quick forge and working-house of thought', had no existence.

Language itself teaches him what he has to say. He gives a Falstaff or a Hamlet, or a Rosalind or Mercutio, their head, and puts at their disposal, as language-creatures, *his* fund of words and allusions, his fantasy, his humour, his capacity to break through to those revelations of insight and feeling that we call 'Shakespearian'. And none of it is fixed. The language-world of *Romeo and Juliet* – and of Romeo or Capulet or Mercutio or the Nurse within it – is not the language-world of *As You Like It*, or of *Henry IV Part I* or *Hamlet*.

Language leads him, as it does any writer. No question of that, but what of his fellow players? Having in sight, as he wrote, the strong physical presence of a Burbage or the inspired clowning of a Will Kemp, was he also inwardly listening to *them*? Was it their voices in his head that carried the words he was setting down, and to this extent transformed what he was creating, as what he was demanding of them must have transformed and extended them?

Consider what Burbage would have been forced to discover in himself as he moved from declarative performance, all exterior gesture, in *Richard III*, where to *be* is to *act* and power over others means quite literally acting them off the stage, to the anxious self-awareness of Hamlet, who moves back and forth between performing to a watching audience inside the play and thinking aloud to an audience outside it.

Did Shakespeare conceive this new focus of drama, and the new style of acting that could represent it, out of the material itself and his own imagination, or was he responding as well to something he saw in

Burbage? A capacity for suggesting inner states; for entering the *mind* as well as capturing the eye and ear of an audience.

These are questions we cannot answer. But given what we know of the collective way in which these companies worked, we in no way diminish Shakespeare's genius by raising them.

*

Play-going in the 1590s, like cinema-going in the 1930s, was cheap popular entertainment with no pretensions to being more; and Hollywood in the thirties, with its studio and star system, might be as good a model as we can light on for the theatre Shakespeare worked in: plays rapidly produced week in week out to serve a regular audience; most of them got together by groups working in collaboration, most of them dispensable and soon lost. Scripts owned by the companies, and the more popular among them jealously guarded in an atmosphere of close rivalry and a scramble to reproduce one another's successes. A general contempt, on the part of the best minds of the day, a Sidney in the 1580s, a Virginia Woolf or F. R. Leavis in the thirties, for a phenomenon that was the preserve of wastrels and apprentices in one case and shopgirls and secretaries in the other. Then, three decades later, the extraordinary discovery that this, at its best, had all along been the great expressive art of the age, and the recognition that what had been taken as routine market products of an industry were in some cases what Jonson called Works, and what the French New Wave critics called the highly individual productions of an 'auteur'.

Difficult to see perhaps at the time because genuine masterpieces like *Hamlet* or *A Midsummer Night's Dream*, or *The Palm Beach Story* or *Double Indemnity*, were produced by the same system, and for the same audience, as *Mucedorus* and *The Stepmother's Tragedy*, or the Hopalong Cassidy or Mexican Spitfire series, and audiences, in each case, were both discriminating and not. But what we know of film-going tells us something very useful about how an audience educates itself into the subtleties of a form. Going to the movies was its own crash-course in movie-going. After just a decade of sound, how skilful an audience had to be to keep up with a fast-moving, fast-talking comedy like *His Girl Friday* or the narrative techniques of a *Citizen Kane*. And all this in the case of an audience that could read but was hardly what we, or a Virginia Woolf, might call literate. Only avid for diversion, for experience, and the rewards, if they learned quickly enough, of laughter, action, spectacle, suspense, tears, surprise, illumination.

Shakespeare has high expectations of his audience. He asks them, as seasoned playgoers, to pick up references to earlier styles and to participate in the high level of by-play this produces – comic in some cases, in others deadly serious.

In Act V, Scene III of *Henry IV, Part II*, Silence, Falstaff and old Justice Shallow have retired to Shallow's orchard for a late drink in what Silence calls 'the sweet of the night'. Suddenly Pistol arrives, hot-foot from the court, knocks at the gate and bursts in among them with his 'good tidings'. But the language in which he delivers them – the bombastic high style of a messenger in an old play – is incomprehensible to his listeners. 'I pray thee now,' Falstaff urges, 'deliver them like a man of *this* world.' But Pistol cannot be brought to earth, and Falstaff sees that if he is to get anything sensible out of him, he must enter Pistol's own language world. 'O base Assyrian knight,' he begs, 'what is thy news? / Let King Cophetua know the truth thereof.'

Shakespeare's point – comic in this case – is that if characters are to communicate with one another they must speak the same language and be in the same play. If they are not the result can be comically absurd but may also, in other circumstances, be fatal.

In *Othello*, for example, the hero's integrity, both dramatically and in his own view of himself, depends on the fixity of his stance and the exalted 'nobility' of his language. In no way analytical as Hamlet is in one way and Macbeth in another – in fact self-regarding rather than self-aware – the language Othello uses is stately, representative, full of the assurance (false as it happens) that words have a fixed and accepted meaning. This is the language of an earlier dramatic style, and by the first decade of the new century was as outdated in its way as Pistol's.

Iago on the other hand belongs to the new world of the City Comedies; he speaks the language of the streets. Words in his mouth are serviceable; they shift their meaning to suit the occasion, and whatever it is that is being exchanged or trafficked.

Iago and Othello are in the same play but belong to language worlds that embody different modes of apprehension and different forms of experience. In any meeting between them in which dialogue or argument rather than action is the instrument, Othello is lost.

Shakespeare's response to the new City Comedy – which he himself had so brilliantly made way for in the Eastcheap scenes in *Henry IV* – was not to challenge Jonson, Rowley, Middleton and the rest by taking it up, but to free it of its local setting, its low-life confidence tricks and high-life swindles, and while retaining its sense of the street and its edge of savage humour, make tragedy of it.

Shakespeare's audience, or that part of it that had been trained by him to be alert to language styles, and awake, like Iago himself, to the pitfalls that are there to be exploited in the nuances of difference, must have been keenly, comically, anxiously aware of what was in operation here, and seen it as part of the play's meaning, as well as the source of those fatal misunderstandings that allow Iago to practise his own half-comic, half-sinister form of 'coney-catching'.

*

Fascinating to observe, from the early plays that have survived under his name, how surely the younger Shakespeare grasped what it was in the mix of popular subjects and styles that engaged and challenged him, but more importantly, fitted his temperament.

He writes, in *The Comedy of Errors* and *The Taming of the Shrew*, two machine-like comedies – small masterpieces in their way – then confidently moves on; tries one Senecan tragedy, sees how much or how little of its sensationalism he might make use of, and again moves on.

What suits him, in the way of comedy, is not at all machine-like; is rather loose in fact, and relies not on situation but on the grouping of characters, high and low, around a set of related questions: love, true or false; love's language, true or false; love painfully concealed or only reluctantly recognised; uneasy wooing; high-spirited warring between the sexes in which men and women are equal – in wit, in desire, in a sense of their own worth; the whole unified by a poetry, sometimes sad, always tender, sweet but lively, in which Renaissance, Classical, and English folk elements all find a place. Darkness is recognised in the shadow of time and mortality, but the mood is essentially one of reconciliation and fulfilment; open to good-humoured mockery, but with little or no place for corrective judgement or moral or social satire.

The style had its day, then went out, replaced by a form of comedy that was crueller, sharper, more relevant, more streetwise. What Shakespeare's form of comedy belonged to was in fact the future: the lighthearted world of the Restoration, the eighteenth- and early nineteenth-century comedy of manners, and what a later age would discover and call Romanticism. Tragedy, of a kind he will make entirely his own, he comes to obliquely, via the English chronicle play.

What the chronicle plays offered was a form of national epic. Moving across classes, trades, counties, it bodied forth the nation in all its degrees, all its variety of types and dialects and accents, and was free, in its loose way, to take up a whole range of complex political questions: kingship, order, rebellion, accident, individual destiny; how far ambition in the great, and the needs of ordinary living in the rest, might need to be negotiated in an ever-changing world; how a place could be found, and a case made, for a Richard II, a Bolingbroke, a Gloucester, a Queen Margaret, but also for a Hotspur, a Falstaff, a Jack Cade, a Mistress

Quickly, a Fluellen, a Justice Shallow, a Bullcalf. No other playwright of the period has so sweeping a vision but finds so much room for engaging minutiae – for Francis the tap-boy's 'anon, anon', the Bishop of Ely's strawberries, the voices of Bates and Williams in the night scene before Agincourt, or, within the world of dazzling display and false show that is *Richard III*, for the still moment that is Clarence's dream.

Clarence's exploration of conscience and the emotional landscape of guilt – as much a matter of *feeling* aloud as of *thinking* aloud – has a different pace from the rest of the play he finds himself in. 'Had you such leisure in the time of death,' the Keeper asks, 'To gaze upon the secrets of the deep?' In pausing to evoke an invisible, interior world, it is at odds with the play's other more headlong and exterior mode and momentum. Which is why – extraordinary as it is – the scene disappeared so early from the text, and even after its restoration in the nineteenth century was till our own time never played. For Shakespeare it is a key moment.

What Clarence opens to view, and dramatises, is that inner world of dreams, of irrational doubts and fears, for which we have our own name: the unconscious. Once Shakespeare grasps how it can be used, how it can be fitted into the unfolding action, the possibility is opened for a new kind of play. The action moves within. Into Hamlet's or Macbeth's other-world of conscience, of a consciousness 'sickled o'er with thought'. And that, now, is where the audience is asked to follow.

What is offered in return is a new closeness: intimacy of a kind that changes what the actor is engaged in from presentation to inward questioning, and the audience's role from spectator to sharer in the actor's most secret thoughts. It is when we come to the Dover scene in *Lear* – Edgar's moment with his father on an imaginary cliff-top, and the manipulation of Gloucester's (and the audience's) vision of it – that we see how far Shakespeare has pushed the notion of 'action' on the stage, and how far he expects his audience to take the leap and follow.

The stage as usual is empty. The audience, again as usual, is dependent on one of the actors to evoke for them, in the word-pictures of which this playwright is the master, an invisible reality, as the Chorus does, for example in *Henry V*, right down to the ship's boys climbing on the tackle of sails, and which is what Edgar appears to be doing here when he describes from far off the 'samphire gatherer' halfway down the cliff.

But Edgar is evoking this scene for a blind man, and if the audience takes the usual cue and believes what it is hearing it will, like the blind man, right up to the moment of Gloucester's leap, be deceived.

This is an extraordinarily daring piece of play

with the usual conventions, and only an audience long skilled in responding and then questioning its response could grasp what is actually happening. At what point, one wonders, did it happen at the play's first performance, and with how much bewilderment or illuminating surprise?

We understand all this because the plays have been with us now, familiar and acceptable, for some 400 years, but also because they, and the mind that shaped them, have shaped our minds to receive them: this is our inheritance. The interiorising modern world we take for granted is the one Shakespeare opened to us. What we might see in the Dover Cliff scene is the sort of experience we ascribe now to the pleasures of reading; which is being offered, in this case, to an audience that could not yet read, or have any notion – save in a moment like this – of what that might be.

One other element of the plays belongs to the future – one perhaps that more than any other humanises and endears them to us.

Nabokov, in praising the novel, speaks of the place its large form allows to the gratuitous, to what he calls 'lovely irrelevancy'. 'What some readers suppose to be trifles not worth stooping to,' he tells us, 'is what literature actually consists of . . . A great writer's world is a magic democracy where . . . even the most incidental character . . . has the right to live and breed.' He is speaking, of course, of the novel, but what he has to say might equally apply to Shakespeare.

Consider this exchange, after some talk about corns and dancing, between the two Capulets in *Romeo and Juliet*:

> *Cap.* Nay, sit, nay, sit, good cousin Capulet,
> For you and I are past our dancing days.
> How long is't now since last yourself and I
> Were at a mask?
> *Cap* 2. By'r Lady, thirty years.
> *Cap.* What man? 'tis not so much, 'tis not so much.
> 'Tis since the nuptial of Lucentio,
> Come Pentecost as quickly as it will,
> Some five and twenty years, and then we masked.
> *Cap* 2. 'Tis more, 'tis more: his son is elder, sir;
> His son is thirty.
> *Cap.* Will you tell me that?
> His son was a ward two years ago.

All this, wonderfully touching and real, entirely irrelevant, in the foreground, at the very moment when Romeo is catching his first glimpse of Juliet. In the very next line he stops a passing servant to ask, 'What lady's that which doth enrich the hand / Of yonder knight?' – one of those over-pressed servants who, as the scene opens, are running to and fro as they bring in the dishes:

Where's Potpan, that he helps not to take away? *He* shift a trencher! *He* scrape a trencher . . . Away with the joint-stools, remove the court-cubben, look to the plate. Good thou, save me a piece of marchpane; and as thou love me let the porter let in Susan Grindstone and Nell. Antony – and Potpan!

Or there are the two stewed prunes (Master Froth having eaten the rest) that Elbow's wife, being great with child, had a longing for, and which stood, 'as it were, in a fruit dish', at Mistress Overdone's, a dish as Pompey explains, 'of some three-pence; your honours have seen such dishes, they are not China dishes, but very good dishes'. 'Go to, go to,' the exasperated Escalus interrupts, who is the judge trying to make sense of all this, 'no matter for the dish, Sir.'

No matter indeed. A trifle not worth stooping to – as Aristotle and his university-trained followers would agree. But it is in just such trifles that the deepest truth of the plays can be found. They let life in; the teeming world of objects in motion from hand to hand that make up the traffic of households, courts, cities. They allow a place for accident and muddle of every sort, and, if only in passing, for the self-absorption and lively self-interest of those who, like the musicians in *Romeo and Juliet*, are no longer wanted once Juliet has been found dead but have some hope still of the funeral sweetmeats, and though they have, strictly speaking, no part in the action, are nevertheless *there*, and once recognised, are allowed their moment on the stage.

What makes all this possible – this indulgence well beyond what might be demanded by 'art' – is a form that knows no rules of exclusion; so open to variety and interest that virtually anything can be crammed in and made germane, for the simple reason that it belongs to *life*. Also, on the author's part, to an eye, an ear, a mind – to go back to Henry James – on which nothing is ever lost; that takes everything in, and finds a time and place for it, and an audience that has been educated, play by play, into sharing this astonishing receptivity and quickness of response.

If I come back, at the end, to the audience, it is because there is a continuity between the audience, as he created it, and us, that it would be presumptuous to claim more directly with the man himself; because learning to respond, as they did, to what he asked them to see and feel – to identify for example, as it is pointed out and made real to a blind man, that samphire-gatherer halfway down the imaginary cliff, and to pause for a moment and consider the dreadfulness of his trade – is the kind of small, irreplaceable experience that only he offers us, and which brings us immediately close to him.

The making of plays was one thing. The re-making of minds to create an audience that would be ready to take them in was another thing again. That audience is us. What we owe him most of all, perhaps, is the capacity he created in us to receive his extraordinary gift.

Address to the World Shakespeare 2006 Congress

A COMPANY OF EGOS

'VICTOR HUGO WAS A madman who thought he was Victor Hugo.' The pungency of Cocteau's *bon mot* lies in its dismissal of the most voluble, the most extravagantly prolific French writer of the nineteenth century in a single sentence. Done!

In nine novels, a dozen plays and more than a thousand poems, Hugo had set out to dominate the language and establish himself, *contra* Racine, as the true voice of the national literature. It was because he was so much larger than life, in his ego, his output, his sexual appetite, and in the power he claimed as the vehicle of advanced opinion, that he came so close to fulfilling his own notion of himself as the grand intersection of all the century's lines of force. But the notion was a crazy one, as the century itself was crazy.

Napoleon, simply by being what he was, had created a *new* type: the man from nowhere – from Corsica or

Tours or Angoulême – who, with none of the advantages of birth or wealth, by sheer force of will, subdues the world to his demands and fashions his own destiny. His career became the prototype for every form of nineteenth-century endeavour. In Balzac's vast panorama of post-revolutionary France, all the dominant figures, from Rastignac on, have Napoleon as their model – Bianchon is the Napoleon of medicine, Vautrin of crime, Derville of the law. Balzac himself, of course, is the Napoleon of literature.

If it was Hugo's madness to imagine he was someone *other* than Napoleon, it was because he took this 'someone other' as embodying more completely than Napoleon had both the spirit of the nation and all the phenomena of the age. For Hugo, the only madness worth aspiring to was to be Victor Hugo. Not for nothing was his crest Ego-Hugo.

How to write the life of such a monster without being Balzac – that is the challenge. Graham Robb has prepared for it by writing the life of Balzac. His *Victor Hugo* is an even grander achievement.

Like Marius in *Les Miserables*, Hugo was the son of a 'Brigand of the Loire', one of Joseph Bonaparte's Spanish generals with the title 'Count of Siquenza'. His mother was also a daughter of the revolution – her grandfather had worked with Jean Carrier, the butcher of Nantes, and one of her aunts was his mistress – but she too was a fantasist and bent the facts a little so that

Hugo could become, in his mythologising of his life as a national drama, the offspring of opposing political forces as well as opposite geographical regions: father a 'republican vandal' from Alsace, mother a 'royalist Amazon' from that heartland of *Chouan* resistance, Brittany.

In the marital civil war that was the background to his youth, Hugo took his mother's part, and to spite the general, again like Marius, became a Catholic royalist. But when his mother died just before his twentieth birthday he resumed relations with his father, made a sudden turn in the old Bonapartist direction and began a life-long flirtation with the Left.

It is Hugo's early friend, the poet Alfred de Vigny, who provides the sharpest commentary on all this:

> The Victor I loved is no more . . . He used to be a touch fantastical in his royalism and his religion, chaste as a girl and rather timid too . . . Now he likes to make saucy remarks and is turning into a liberal . . . He started out mature and is entering on his youth, living after writing, whereas one ought to write after living.

Vigny's portrait allows us a revealing glimpse as well of the young Hugo's amazing precocity.

At sixteen, the winner of the Académie Française's prize for poetry, he was taken up by the court and made himself, through a series of celebratory odes, its unofficial laureate; he became 'official' seven years later, in 1825. In a burst of creative energy that has much to do, one suspects, with the pressures of a dedicated virginity, he produced, before he was twenty-one, two works of fiction (the first version of *Bug-Jargal* and *Han d'Islande*), 112 articles and two volumes of odes and ballads. Vigny is scathing about Hugo's method of educating himself 'by going about from one man to another and helping himself to whatever they have to offer': Sainte-Beuve, Charles Nodier (from whom the Angel-Victor of the 1820s also picked up his later and rather scabrous bohemian style), his brother Abel. But how else is a young man to educate himself? The point is not what a writer steals but what he makes of it. What Hugo stole on most occasions was the thunder. *Hernani* was not the first drama to break the rules of unity and play fast and loose with the alexandrine, but it was the one that drew a rag-tag, noisy audience and created a riot at the sacred site of French classical drama, the Comédie Française. So, too, most of what appears in the preface to *Cromwell* had already been said by others, but it was Hugo's rhetoric that made it a classic text.

By 1830 Hugo, not yet thirty, was at once the darling of a fuddy-duddy court, a Romantic rebel and a budding republican. When his father died in 1831 he refashioned himself as Baron Hugo, insisting thus on his father's place in the Imperial nobility as opposed to that of the Ancien Régime or the new Bourbons – a distinction essential, as readers of Balzac will know, to the snobberies but also to the ideological affinities of the period. Hugo would get a title in his own right when he became a *pair de France* in 1845. But by then he was on the way to mystical socialism.

Robb writes that 'Hugo's childhood had not been the plot of a melodrama', though one might mistake it for one, 'but a series of contradictory certainties'. This goes some way perhaps to explaining Hugo's fawning attempts to get himself elected to that Parnassus of literary respectability, the Académie Française, while at the same time plotting, as *enfant terrible* of the Romantic movement, to destroy it; and why each step he took up the ladder of nobility was accompanied by a sidestep to the Left.

As for more intimate matters: Hugo's sexual adventures, once he had offered up his virginity, are legendary. The last remaining connotation of the term Hugoesque in English, as Robb sadly notes, is an entry in the *Oxford English Dictionary* of 1960: 'Almost Hugoesque in his unflagging pursuit of maids.' One suspects that if Hugo's encounters with women had been recorded in his diary in erotic detail rather than minimalist code, they might rival Walter's in *My Secret Life*. He was, like Walter, like Dickens too, a night wanderer, an explorer after midnight of the city's dark underparts. We also know, because he tells us, that he had his first 'adult' erection at nine, and was still noting the phenomenon at seventy-nine; that he took his wife nine times on their wedding night and was once complimented on the same achievement, some years later, by his mistress of fifty years, Juliette Drouet. A speech in the Assembly, he tells us with his usual lack of humour about such matters, 'is as exacting as ejaculating three times, even four'. His pet name for his penis, nicely marking the correspondence for him between sexual activity and writing, was 'my lyre'. Yet all the significant figures in his fiction, Frollo, Quasimodo, Esmeralda, Marius and the various young men who die on the barricades in *Les Misérables*, even Jean Valjean and Javert, are virgins.

Dealing with all this, if Hugo is not to emerge as either a pathological self-deceiver or a blatant liar, is a matter of negotiating the contradictions, and it is best if, like Robb, you have a flair for paradox and prefer definition by metaphor to psychoanalysis (though the temptation, given the younger Hugo's obsession with hunchbacks and red-headed dwarfs, must have been considerable). So Robb can write: 'In Hugo's moral universe, there was sometimes little difference between an act of cowardice and an act of courage; both meant ignoring the usual code of conduct.'

This seems to me to get the man right. It sounds like Hugo, who defined boredom as a state in which 'life seems entirely logical'; who, when asked the point of *Les Orientales*, in which he had discovered for poetry a process in which language itself drives the poem, replied: 'The author has no idea . . . He has never seen any roadmaps of Art, with the frontiers of the possible and the impossible drawn in red and blue.' Or to choose two other examples, both of an astonishing modernity: 'As a person one is sometimes a stranger to what one writes as a poet'; and 'All great writers create two oeuvres, one deliberate, one involuntary.'

As Robb suggests, referring to the adjustments by which Hugo made it appear that key works such as *Hernani* and *Notre-Dame de Paris* coincided with and may even have precipitated revolutionary events: 'These lies are probably closer to the truth that matters than accurate statements. By adjusting his chronology, Hugo was hinting that though he himself may have been deaf to the evidence, his works had already known that he was on the side of the masses.'

Hugo, in Robb's generous view, is like some early example of multiple personality disorder, 'not just a real person with several masks, but a limited liability company of egos, each one feeding off the other and maintained by an army of commentators'. He even offers a kind of answer to Cocteau. 'Everyone is a lunatic in the privacy of their own mind, and, considering the treasures in Hugo's unconscious, his apparent sanity is a far more remarkable phenomenon.'

And the works? We can, each one, have no more than a fragmentary response to that vast outpouring: to *Notre-Dame*, *Les Misérables* and *Les Travailleurs de la Mer* read in early adolescence; to plays discovered through favourite operas; to poems such as 'Oceano Nox' and 'Les Djinns', learned by heart at school, and others read in a more general way later, 'Booz endormi', 'A Villequier', 'Demain dès l'aube'.

When we read out of another language, out of French or German or Russian, what emerges in us is another reader. Life in that other order of experience – the way objects there are related to the senses, the balance between public and private selves, the part sex plays in one's image of oneself, to name only a few aspects of the thing – all this is sufficiently different to call up a self we may never come upon if we read only in our native tongue.

I began to grasp something of this when I first read *The Count of Monte Cristo*. I was ten, maybe eleven. Soon afterwards my parents bought me a whole set of Dumas, twenty volumes in morocco leather; I read them all, one after another, and went on quickly to *René*, *Atala*, *Paul et Virginie*, and after seeing the Charles Laughton film, to *Notre-Dame*.

What these books offered an over-imaginative pre-adolescent, beyond sensational plots and another version of history, was something I had not encountered till then: the stimulation of a side of my nature, all the more potent for being unspecific, that kept me in a state of almost continuous physical excitement.

Sometimes the appeal was sadistic, as in an early chapter of *La Tulipe Noire* (my only other response of this kind was when, at sixteen, I got to the end of that orgy of erotic delights, *Salammbô*). I was disturbed, a little frightened even, by my own excitement. But it was something closer to normality, *La Reine Margot* I remember, that hit me hardest. Finishing it under the bedclothes at night, I had a fit of hysterical weeping and was forbidden any more of these secret readings – though not, oddly enough, the reading itself. Only one book was forbidden, *La Dame aux Camélias*. I read it, of course, and was disappointed. The sex there was overt and what I had been reading for was something different – the over-all sexiness of eroticism: erotic *subtext*. Best of all for that was *Notre-Dame*.

Intriguing, then, to discover that Hugo called reason 'intelligence taking exercise' and imagination 'intelligence with an erection'. Also to hear from Robb that 'Hugo's most successful relationships were with people under the age of ten' (that is, as sexually awake as he was at nine, but immature) 'or with the ten-year-old parts of their personality'.

The erotic subtext of *Notre-Dame* is still strong – it is as if Hugo were writing in a state of continuous arousal – but the adult reader will find its real interest elsewhere: in the comic lightness of the first hundred pages, which mainly follow Gringoire, and especially in the Rabelaisian grotesquerie of the Court of Miracles; even more in the essayistic chapters that follow: 'Notre-Dame' and 'A Bird's-Eye View of Paris', with its lyrical coda on the bells: 'Ordinarily the murmur that escapes from Paris in the daytime is the city talking; in the night it is the city breathing; but here it is the city singing. Listen, then, to the tutti of the steeples.'

Most dazzling of all is the chapter called 'This Will Kill That', on the displacement of the ancient and medieval worlds by the modern, and of architecture by the printing press. It is here that we see Hugo's astonishing energy and originality as he throws off idea after idea that will be essential to the new way of perceiving. 'When a man understands the art of seeing,' he writes, 'he can trace the spirit of the age even in the knocker on a door.' This is the Hugo who, travelling for the first time by train, in 1841, sees immediately that travelling at speed changes and disintegrates everything we look at, and so becomes one of the precursors of impressionism.

This capacity for experiencing from within is everywhere in *Notre-Dame*. In an act of bold appropriation, he takes a mouldy, unfashionable half-ruin and brings it to life again, but in a new form: cathedral as book. Its silhouette, H, becomes his personal monogram. He

enters its stone life (partly through the double identi-
fication with Quasimodo) and re-creates it as text. He
occupies and makes it, this monument at the heart of
Paris (as he had already made the Comédie Française
and would in time make the Académie, the Assemblé,
the Place des Vosges and at last even the Panthéon), a
monument to himself; proving his thesis that This Will
Kill That by replacing stone with a print work whose
multilingual inscriptions and private references antici-
pate Ruskin, Proust and a host of twentieth-century
theorists, and make Eco look like a lazy schoolboy. In
the light of all this, even the descent into the underworld of nightmare and folklore out of which he drew
Quasimodo, impressive as it is, seems like child's play.

And the plot?

One of the revolutions wrought by Romanticism,
which came late to France – they were occupied with
changes of another sort – was in the nature of the
audience. The real scandal of *Hernani* was the inva-
sion of the Comédie Française by an audience of the
people, and it was this new audience, with its own
ideas of what would please, that changed the nature
of writing in the 1830s.

The problem for the novelist who needed to *sell* (not
Stendhal, of course, who clung proudly to the Happy
Few) was how to reconcile the sensational requirements
of a new readership, the general reading public, with
serious literary values. Balzac did this by fashioning

his plots out of intrigue, deception, and by making the pursuit of sex, power and commercial advantage – from the top to the bottom of society, as the Human Comedy presents it – forms of the same vital force. The Brontës took the Gothic and domesticated it, transposing its mysterious, supernatural elements to the landscape or weather and making 'love' a kind of possession or haunting. Dickens, most powerfully of all, used co-incidence and revelation to lay bare, under the ordinary fabric of society, a set of hidden relationships where what defined and linked his characters was not family or class but old half-forgotten passions, crimes or even darker, more secret affinities.

And Hugo? One of the inscriptions on a wall of Notre Dame is the Greek word 'ΑΝΑΓΚΗ' – fate.

In Hugo, all the major characters are linked by what he would have us believe is destiny. So Quasimodo is the baby monster left in place of Sachette's stolen child, Esmeralda, and when Frollo decides to adopt him it is because he is thinking at the moment of his baby brother, Jehan. Esmeralda, Quasimodo and Jehan are fatally related and This Will Kill That – in a way that is shocking enough, but entirely gratuitous.

Nothing in Hugo happens naturally. It is all stage-managed by a God called Hugo, a sanctimonious old ruffian who will not let his characters go. And everything in Hugo is built on antithesis – a stylistic device, he reminds us, that God also uses. Light/dark, male/female – so why not beauty/ugliness, saint/sinner, policeman/criminal?

'Valjean,' he tells us, 'had this trait, that he might be said to carry two knapsacks – in the one he had the thoughts of a saint, in the other the impressive talents of a convict.' But these two sides of Valjean belong to geometry rather than psychology, they are neither in conflict nor in alliance; and Valjean is less a victim of society, or fate, or mischance, than of the plot Hugo has fabricated around him, which he has to use all his talents to escape. He is no more complex in the end than his nemesis Javert, that barbarian in the service of civilisation who, when he discovers that Valjean is not simply a convict, has no other recourse, his oppositional view of the world having entirely disintegrated, than to drown himself.

Very different is that other great fictional convict of the period, Balzac's Vautrin, whose genius for disguise and transformation, for entering into the soul of others – as idle man of affairs, Spanish cardinal, Mephistophelian seducer of naïve but ambitious young men – makes him the prime mover of his world, its great manipulator and *vengeur*. In his last incarnation (no easy antithesis here) he himself becomes the law, in the form of chief of the Parisian police, a role for which, in Balzac's cynical view, his criminal career is the ideal preparation. This sort of playfulness and subversive provocation is beyond Hugo. Vigny, one feels, was right. After the brilliant maturity of his youth (*Le Dernier Jour d'un Condamné, Notre-Dame*) he declined into shallow youthfulness, fell into what Balzac – that Catholic royalist who was also the favourite novelist of Lukács and Marx – called 'the democratic vertigo to which so many blind writers succumb'; became the universal signer of petitions and supporter of freedom fighters in every part of the globe; the first pan-European; courageous opponent of the death penalty, slavery, the Church and every form of ignorance; passionate believer that universal education, 'identical schools, Light, Light!' would eradicate all the injustices and evils of society, indeed evil itself – a 'sublime cretin' (Dumas *fils*), 'stupid as the Himalayas' (Leconte de Lisle) – who when he died at eighty-three was the best-known citizen of our planet.

And the future he hailed in such glowing terms? ('Citizens, the nineteenth-century is great but the twentieth-century will be happy . . . War will be dead; the scaffold, hate, royalty, frontiers and dogmas will all be dead.') Well, we have seen that. We are living with it. It is Auschwitz, Bosnia, the Gulags, Rwanda, *Les Miz*, and the best guide to its splendours and miseries, its vulgarity, its follies, its cruelties great and small, is the best guide we have to Hugo's century as well, the author of *La Comédie Humaine*.

The Australian Review of Books, *1997*

READING THE SIGNS: *JANE EYRE*

THERE ARE SOME BOOKS that make such a vivid impression on us, put us so deeply under their spell, that our first acquaintance with them becomes a watershed in our lives and the actual reading – the excited turning of pages over a period of hours or days – seems in retrospect to have taken place in a country all its own, with a light and weather like no other we have ever known.

I read *Jane Eyre* in the Christmas holidays – the long summer break – between primary and secondary school; I was not quite thirteen. Some of it I read slumped in a canvas chair on our beach-house verandah, within sound of the surf; some of it on the beach itself between swims. What extraordinary creatures we are that we can be, on the same occasion, in two quite different places; and what a business reading is that fifty years after the event the landscape of Thornfield in the frost, as I first came upon it, is as present in my memory as the hot sands of Main Beach Southport and my own body under the blazing sun. What did I get from the book that it should have hit so hard?

The voice of the narrator, first of all, which once you have given yourself up to it is irresistible; so close, so much part of your own inner world that everything Jane sees and feels is immediately a revelation. It is as if you had discovered the key not just to a book but to the world – a world full of signs to be read, and inter-connections you had not previously imagined.

One of those interconnections is between individuals. Ardently romantic, the announcement of it comes to the adolescent of either sex as a lightning flash.

'He is not of their kind,' Jane tells herself of Mr Rochester, rejecting at a stroke all the circumstances that divide them. 'I believe he is of mine; I am sure he is, – I feel akin to him, – I understand the language of his countenance and movements; though rank and wealth sever us widely, I have something in my brain and heart, in my blood and veins, that assimilates me mentally to him.'

Rousing stuff, this bold assertion of the primacy of feeling, this sympathy between souls that can leap across real space as well as social barriers, and is grounded in the physical but can so immediately transcend it. Jane is not even in solitude when she hears the voice of Mr Rochester calling to her out of the night. 'The one candle was dying out: the room was full of moonlight. My heart beat fast and thick: I heard its throb. Suddenly it stood still to an inexpressible feeling that filled it through, and passed at once to my head and extremities. The feeling was not like an electric shock; but it was quite as sharp, as strange, as startling: it acted on my senses as if their utmost activity hitherto had been but torpor; from which they were now summoned, and forced to wake. They rose expectant: eye and ear waited, while the flesh quivered on my bones.'

One of the things that convinces us most in this passage is that in describing the state in which Mr Rochester's voice comes to her, the words Jane finds, in their rhythm, in the intensity with which the physical and the mental become one, reproduce just the state in which Jane's voice, as narrator, comes to us. We believe utterly in the form of sympathy she proposes because we ourselves are the subject of it.

Late in the book, Jane pictures the world as a network of such correspondences or sympathies – between individual souls, between individuals and what they produce – her pictures, for example, which Mr Rochester takes as clues to her inner world – between events in the human sphere and their reflection in Nature. Interpreting the world is a matter of reading 'signs'. 'Presentiments are strange things!' Jane tells us. 'And so are sympathies; and so are signs: and the three combined make one mystery of which humanity has not yet found the key.'

As for the tale she has to tell, Jane is so sympathetically attuned to the events of it that they seem at times to be no more than a projection of her own intimate yearning. She stands, as a narrator, somewhere between Catherine Morland of Jane Austen's *Northanger Abbey*, whose thinking is so conditioned by the sensational novels she has absorbed that she mistakes the oddness of people, and the strangeness of real life, for the making of yet another Gothic fiction, and that other governess and servant of an absent master, the anonymous narrator of Henry James' *The Turn of the Screw* – 'young, untried, nervous' – whose account of the 'mysteries' at Bly hovers so ambiguously on the edge of neurotic fantasy.

There is no ambiguity in Jane's case. In her down-to-earth way she resists the suggestion that Thornfield may house a mystery. But the world of story – 'Passages of love and adventure taken from old fairytales and other ballads or (as at a later period I discovered) from Pamela' – has a strong influence on what she has to tell.

Writing of her free hours, she tells us: 'The restlessness was in my nature . . . Then my sole relief was to walk along the corridor of the third storey, backwards and forwards, safe in the silence and solitude of the spot, and allow my mind's eye to dwell on whatever bright visions rose before it . . . and, best of all, to open my inward ear to a tale that was never ended – a tale my imagination created, and narrated continuously; quickened with all of incident, life, fire, feeling, that I desired and had not in my actual existence.'

The place Jane chooses for her reveries, the corridor of the third storey, is itself significant, though she does not as yet know it. 'One would almost say,' Mrs Fairfax tells her, 'that, if there were a ghost at Thornfield Hall, this would be its haunt.'

There is no ghost, but Jane, with her usual prescience, does see something. 'With its two rows of small black doors all shut,' it is 'like a corridor in some Bluebeard's castle'. When, later, she sits alone at dusk on the stile in Hay Lane, and hears the approach of hooves, 'all sorts of fancies', she tells us, 'bright and dark tenanted my mind: the memories of nursery stories were there amongst other rubbish'.

The sturdy common sense of that 'amongst other rubbish' speaks for the side of Jane's nature that is suspicious of mysteries and of the irrational. The dash of cold water it provides (quite literally and comically in the case of Mr Rochester's bed) is meant to save her from falling into Catherine Morland's error; whereas it is only by accepting the irrational, and making a place for the extreme, that she might have discovered, behind Grace Poole with her 'pot of porter', the even darker figure of Mrs Rochester. She even misreads the events in Hay Lane. 'The incident had occurred and was gone for me: it was an incident of no moment, no romance, no interest in a sense.'

This is plain Jane speaking. Closer to the truth is the Jane who, just before the appearance of her phantom rider, remembers 'certain of Bessie's tales wherein figured a North-of-England spirit . . . which, in the form of a horse, mule, or large dog, haunted solitary ways . . .'

This spirit first takes the form of a dog, Mr Rochester's mastiff, Pilot, then of a horse and rider, and though 'The man, the human being, broke the spell at once', her apparition, her demon lover, continues to inhabit a form halfway between animal and human. When a voice tells her to stand aside, 'I did,' she says, 'whereupon began a heaving, stamping, clattering process, accompanied by a barking and baying'.

The spell of Bessie's tale is not quite broken, and it is part of the erotic power of Jane's narrative that Mr Rochester continues to carry into later episodes a hint, in Jane's mind as in ours, of the Beast of fairytale and folk-story who must be transformed back into a man.

Jane first discovers Mr Rochester's presence at Thornfield when she finds his surrogate, Pilot, on the sitting-room rug, and it is, as she later tells him, not a philtre but the magic of a 'loving eye' that makes him 'human' again, though it is part of the book's tenacious hold on reality that Jane is no Beauty and

Mr Rochester no Prince. 'I had hardly ever seen a handsome youth,' she tells us at her first sight of him, 'never in my life spoken to one. I had a theoretical reverence and homage for beauty, elegance, gallantry, fascination; but had I met those qualities incarnate in masculine shape, I should have known instinctively that they neither had, nor could have sympathy for anything in me.'

There it is again: 'sympathy'. Jane – plain-looking, plain-spoken, 'original'; no more a conventionally attractive young woman than she was, to her aunt, a conventionally acceptable child – is perfectly fitted to this ugly, cross-grained man, whose 'savage' nature disguises surprising gentleness.

With no previous experience to go on she hits immediately on the style of flirtation by which he may be caught, so that when, at the end of their first conversation, the word 'coquetry' drops into the text – in relation to Adèle's perfectly conventional little imitation of it – we have confirmed what we have already understood: that Jane's refusal to play the submissive Victorian maiden, even to a man who is paying her thirty pounds a year, is her own form of coquetry, and the most effective form of it she could have hit upon.

What she does not see is that in failing to present him with a 'ladylike submission and turtledove sensitivity', in answering back so boldly, and allowing him to speak to her of his 'opera mistresses', she has led

Mr Rochester to believe that she may also be willing to *act* unconventionally. He is looking for a woman who will follow him in intentions 'that require a new stature to legalise them', and this of course Jane will not do.

Meanwhile, any haunting that takes place in the book is by the ghosts these lovers find in one another.

He pretends to believe that it is a faery child he has found on the stile in Hay Lane, and when she comes back from Gateshead and confesses that she has been with her aunt, 'who is dead', Mr Rochester replies playfully: 'Good angels be my guard. She comes from another world . . . If I dared, I'd touch you, to see if you are of substance or shadow, you elf!' (Only a moment earlier, when she came upon him, Jane's first thought had been: 'Well, he is not a ghost; yet every nerve I have is unstrung.')

When later they sit alone at supper together, she tells him, 'You, sir, are the most phantom-like of all: you are a mere dream.'

Dreams, premonitions, sympathies, signs . . .

Jane draws the portrait of her rival and anti-self, Blanche Ingram, before she has even laid eyes on her; she sees in a dream the burnt-out shell of Thornfield; 'Bride' is one of the clues, and 'Bridewell' (prison) the solution, in the game of charades Mr Rochester's guests engage in after dinner, but Jane's attention is elsewhere and she misses what all this might reveal to her of the larger mystery. The moth that catches Mr Rochester's eye in the Eden-like orchard on Midsummer's Eve, where he proposes to Jane, is like 'a West Indian insect', and the chestnut tree under which they make their vows, in a sudden shift of the weather, is struck by lightning, though the riven trunk, as Jane later discovers, still has shoots of green.

These 'signs' either enlighten Jane or mislead her according to whether she follows one side or the other of her nature. They are also the signs that we must interpret as readers; part of the book's brilliantly controlled suspense. But the deeper source of our suspense is the concern we feel for Jane herself.

Charlotte Brontë places Jane at the extreme edge of the social world. Orphaned and dependent, she is 'less than a servant' at Gateshead because she does nothing for her keep, and, as a governess, as Charlotte Brontë knew from bitter experience, she is in the anomalous position at Thornfield of being both a paid servant and a 'lady'. All this makes her acutely sensitive to every sort of injustice.

'Unjust – unjust!' she cries in the first pages of the book, and it is typical of her that she should speak out both for Blanche Ingram and Bertha Rochester when she believes Mr Rochester has failed to consider their feelings or their rights.

In the most extreme of the book's moves after her flight from Thornfield, Jane falls out of the safe net of society into that homeless and unsettled space between houses that is the abode of Wordsworth's beggars and of vagrant women like Alice Brown in *Dombey and Son*. She is saved by a couple of narrative ploys that belong to an altogether inferior sort of fiction, but Brontë recovers, and so does Jane. Faced with a subtle temptation to become conventionally submissive, she resists 'the flame and excitement of self-sacrifice', and with her old 'un-feminine' candour, tells St John Rivers, that embodiment of genuine Christian virtue and soft male tyranny: 'If I were to marry you, you would kill me. You are killing me now.'

What saves her is not only the strong sense of her own worth, but also her experience of what love really is.

'He pressed his hand firmer on my head, as if he claimed me,' she writes of Rivers; 'he surrounded me with his arm, almost as if he loved me (I say almost – I knew the difference – for I had felt what it was to be loved . . .).'

After 150 years this speaks as plainly and as directly to the reader as when it was written, and powerfully addresses – even now, when relations between women and men are more open and equal – questions about true feeling and the use of power that have still, in every case, to be negotiated.

No other Victorian novel, not even *David Copperfield*, presents us with a childhood and schooldays more fully realised. No death-bed in Victorian literature is seen with a truer and less sentimental eye than that of Aunt Reed. No other novel in the language has produced so many offspring: from *The Turn of the Screw* ('was there a "secret" at Bly . . . an unmentionable relative kept in unsuspected confinement?'), to Jean Rhys' *Wide Sargasso Sea* and *Rebecca*.

Somewhere on a scorching beach, or tucked up in a sickbed, a young reader, for whom this book is just what they have been waiting for, is about to begin the first sentence of what will be one of the great reading experiences of their life. 'There was no possibility of taking a walk that day.' Their whole world is about to change.

Introduction to Jane Eyre, *Oxford Classics, 1998*

'DRIFT, WAIT, AND OBEY': KIPLING AND THE GREAT GAME

'KIPLING STRIKES ME PERSONALLY as the most complete man of genius (as distinct from fine intelligence) that I have ever known.'

This is Henry James writing to his brother in 1892. Kipling was by then the author of *Plain Tales from the Hills*, *Life's Handicap* (for the first American edition of which, under the title *Mine Own People*, James had provided a preface), a series of six Railway Books, including *Under the Deodars*, *Wee Willie Winkie* and *Soldiers Three*, and a book of *Barrack Room Ballads*. He had survived his first period in London, which he hated, as the literary wonder of the day, had had a nervous breakdown, fled, married the sister of his recently deceased friend and collaborator Wolcott Balestier, and was about to settle in his wife's home town of Brattleboro, Vermont. He was twenty-six.

Writing again, five years later, after the two *Jungle*

Books and *A Day's Work*, James is altogether less enthusiastic:

> My view of his prose future has much shrunken in the light of one's increasingly observing how little life he can make use of. Almost nothing civilised save steam and patriotism . . . Almost nothing of the complicated soul or the female form or any other question of *shades* . . . In his earliest time I thought he perhaps contained the seeds of an English Balzac; but I have given up in proportion as he has come down steadily from the simple in subject to the more simple – from Anglo-Indians to the natives, from the natives to the Tommies, from the Tommies to the quadrupeds, from the quadrupeds to the fish and from fish to engines and screws.

James of course is revealing his own limitations here, as well as Kipling's. But beyond the snobberies both social and aesthetic, and its failure I think to recognise what Kipling does that is unique, this is a criticism that stands, and is worth starting from if we are to make anything of Kipling's achievement.

It is true: Kipling does not, by James' standards, have a fine intelligence, or even, as *The Light That Failed*, his one essay at the novel of feeling, makes plain, a fine sensibility. He is too impatient, too extrovert, for those investigations into the complicated soul that James looks for in a fiction that claims to be art, and of which he himself is the undisputed master. Kipling's world is the masculine world of doing and making, with its codes of honour and daring, respect for professional expertise, loyalty, even affection of a rough sort, but little opportunity for what James calls 'shades'.

It is Kipling's being himself a maker and doer, a product not of one of the great public schools like his cousin Stanley Baldwin but of the United Services College, Westward Ho, a school founded for the training of practical men, the engineers and magistrates who were to serve as second-stringers in the management of the Raj, that leads Kipling to a character such as Findlayson of 'The Bridge Builders' and Hitchcock ('a magistrate of the third class, with whipping powers'), his young second-in-command, and made Kipling, as *McAndrew's Hymn* puts it, the bard of 'Man the Artifax', master of what H. G. Wells called 'shop as a poetic dialect'.

A writer's strengths and weaknesses are one. It is Kipling's 'philistinism', his having no time as a colonial outsider for the niceties of English politeness and good form – his 'hooliganism' as his detractors called it – that allows him to enter without apology, and with no sense of stepping down, into the lives of Ortheris, Learoyd and Mulvaney, the soldiers three, or the young scamps who, in an act of exemplary bravado, sacrifice themselves to regimental honour in 'The Drums of the Fore and Aft'. It is his eye, his 'native' eye, for the sights and sounds and smells and colours of the great subcontinent, the particularities, as we see in *Kim*, of 'how such a caste talked, or walked, or coughed, or spat, or sneezed', his ear, in so much noisy interchange, for idiom and accent, the witticisms, and insults and curses of Tommies, street-vendors, beggars in the native bazaars, that gives his creation of British India – and it is a creation, not a piece of reportage – an energy that must have ripped like a tornado through the lilies and languors of pre-Raphaelite England; a fictional world like nothing else in our literature except Dickens' London, that in the popular mind at least has replaced the original and become the site of its own mythology and truth.

When Henry James sees in his list of Kipling's narrowing interests a dehumanising tendency, a turning away from 'life', he misses the point, I think. One might equally see it as a widening of his sympathies beyond man and his affairs to take in the whole of creation, a capacity to enter not only into the lives of the creatures but into the life energy that is all things; a form of animism that might run counter to what James sees as 'civilisation' but is not necessarily beyond civilised interest, and in Kipling's case goes back to what was deepest in his experience of India itself.

We have only to recall what Forster's finer intelligence made of the same material to see how much more inclusive, how much richer and less judgemental Kipling is; how much of nature, and life and living he is prepared to take in and give voice to. It is the bridge-builder Findlayson – occupied in his confrontation with Mother Gunga (the Ganges) only with piers and spans and girders, with 'remembering, comparing, estimating and re-calculating, lest there be any mistakes' – who is granted access, in an opium dream, to the whole procession of Indian gods in their animal forms as Elephant, Ape, Tiger, Mugger, etc.

And for all his fineness of feeling, Forster is not open, as Kipling is, to the delicacy – which is in fact not so deeply hidden under the rough, uneducated exterior – that allows Mulvaney, of 'Love o' Women', 'The Courtship of Dinah Shand', 'My Lord the Elephant', to recognise, through a form of fellow feeling, a sense of outraged honour in a rampaging jungle beast.

Kipling may not have a fine intelligence, but he does see fineness of feeling in something more than a single class.

It is the openness of Kipling's writing self, his 'daemon' as he calls it, to pre-intellectual, pre-social modes of apprehension that allows him, like Dickens, to create fictions that have the shape, and the dark power of suggestion, the cruelty too at times, of folktales and dreams.

*

The comparison with Dickens is worth pursuing. Both men were insomniacs, obsessively haunted by nightmares that in each case went back to a childhood trauma he had never outgrown.

Dickens at twelve had joined the vast horde of Victorian child labourers, and, with little hope of ever finding his way back to the safe domestic world that had so abruptly cast him out, spent five months in a London blacking factory. Kipling, at just six, was sent 'home' to England with his three-year-old sister Trix, and, with no preparatory explanation, abandoned as he saw it to what he calls 'the House of Desolation' at Southsea, where over the next five and a half years he was regularly abused and even tortured. The story in which he gives an account of this, 'Baa Baa Black Sheep', where he and his sister appear as Punch and Judy – it was more than forty years before he acknowledged that it was his own story – finds a happy ending in family reunion: 'There! I told you so,' says Punch. 'It's all different now, and we are just as much mother's as if she had never gone.' But Kipling's truer writing-self declines to accept it: 'Not altogether Punch,' he adds in a final word, 'for when young lips have drunk deep of the bitter waters of Hate, Suspicion, and Despair, all the Love in the world will not wholly take away the knowledge; though it may turn dark eyes for a while to the light, and teach Faith where no Faith was.'

The works of both writers are crowded with lost or abandoned children: Oliver Twist, Charley Bates, the Artful Dodger; young David Copperfield, the Marchioness of *The Old Curiosity Shop* and Jo in *Bleak House*; young Bailey of *Martin Chuzzlewit*; in Kipling, Punch, the little drummers of the Fore and Aft, Mowgli, even Kim. These children survive, if they do, by internalising the damage that has been done to them and mastering so completely the manners and jargons of their world as to pass – at least outwardly – as confident and sometimes over-confident insiders like the rest.

And both writers of course achieved an early and instant fame (Kipling as perhaps the first writer in English to become an international celebrity whose every deed and word was 'news'), and paid for it with critical disdain.

Dickens recently has been forgiven. Kipling, more disobligingly contrary, has not, though he continues, I'd guess, to be one of the most widely read of English writers; his admirers include T. S. Eliot, Auden and Peter Porter, and Borges thought his later stories surpassed those of Kafka and Henry James.

What remains unforgivable in him is his political stance. For all his egalitarianism (like Dickens his work crosses all the boundaries of class, and relies largely on low-life characters), Kipling was from first to last dismissive of all those forms of liberalism that he saw as the received ideas of his time, and compulsory if one wanted, as he did not, to be taken as enlightened and forward-looking. Kipling's daemon, which he trusted absolutely, was of its nature regressive; pre-Enlightenment, pre-Christian, pre-social; sometimes brutal, often vengeful, and given to cruel practical jokes. Like so much that is most original in him, this too has its roots in his earliest childhood, and in 'India'.

*

Kipling had two Indian periods. We get a good idea of the first from the early pages of *Something of Myself*, his rather desultory attempt, towards the end of his life, at an autobiography:

> In the afternoon heats, before we took our sleep, she [the ayah] or Meeta would tell us stories and Indian Nursery Songs all unforgotten, and we were sent to the dining-room after we had been dressed with the caution, 'Speak English now to Papa and Mama.' So we spoke English haltingly, translated out of the vernacular idiom that one thought and dreamt in.

Such was Kipling's life till he was six; almost the whole of his sensory experience, and everything that fed his childish imagination, picked up in a 'native' way in

Hindi, the language he thought and dreamt in, by a small boy with an extraordinary capacity to take in all that came to him, and a memory that would be coloured forever by the light, the atmosphere, the scenes, the sounds of the world as he first encountered it.

Nothing of England, or English nursery songs and stories, or the English Bible. He tells us quite specifically in 'Baa Baa Black Sheep' that he had never heard of Hell, or 'the vindictive Christian God', till he experienced the first in the House of Desolation and the second at the hands of the woman he calls 'Auntirosa', who took it upon herself, as a good Evangelical Christian, to save her small charge from heathenism, his spoiled boy's assumption of his own importance, and his imagination, which was in her view an addiction to serial lying.

Kipling came unwillingly to Christianity, and among what he thought of as torments. As an Englishman he is a late convert. He never liked England or the English; the Empire, in his vision of it, was meant to save the English from themselves.

Kipling's second period in India came ten years after the first, and began when, at sixteen years and seven months (that is, while he was still young enough to absorb all he came across with the appetite and quickness of youth), he became sub-editor of the *Lahore Civil and Military Gazette*.

As a bright young newspaper man and Sahib, he

had access to all the nooks and crannies of a large garrison town, spending his days, and a good part of his nights, in messes, clubs, liquor shops, opium dens, brothels, but also in native street-markets and temples, gathering all the intelligence he needed for his newspaper work and all the observed life, and folk-lore and gossip, that over the next seven years would go into *Plain Tales from the Hills* and the Railway Books, and later into *Life's Handicap*, *A Diversity of Creatures* and *Kim*.

The result of all this is that Kipling's apprehension of India came in two quite different forms: an earlier intuitive one, picked up without thought as it were in the vernacular – the experience of a 'native' – and a later one that was acquired in adolescence by a trained observer, an outsider but with a native's grasp of the 'why' as he puts it in *Kim*, as well as the 'what' and 'how'.

It is this double view of India, and his gift from Allah of what he calls 'the two sides of my head', that Kipling employs with such brilliance in *Kim*.

Few readers of *Kim* can resist its extraordinary freshness, the sense the writing gives of being awake, like its young hero, Kimball O'Hara, the Little Friend of all the World, 'in a great good-tempered world'. For once the orphan is not an abandoned child but a little free-wheeling adventurer, streetwise, at home with every caste or class, skilled at every sort of exchange and banter, who has cast himself adrift to see what Mother India has to offer him. We can ignore the book's plot, such as it is, and fix our attention, as in any other version of the picaresque, on the various journeys our young hero undertakes and those who share the road with him.

Kim, with his two natures, native and Sahib, is an agent of two worlds: one is represented by the Department in which, as a secret agent of the Great Game, he will one day have a place and number; the other is the world of eternal forms in which even his name, Kim, Kim, Kim, is a mystery to him. At one moment, and in one skin, he is entirely absorbed by 'the visible effects of action', the perfect agent in the book of Kipling's own activity as a writer. In the next, since he, like Kipling, has 'two sides to his head', equally at home in his other, his 'sleeping' nature:

> 'Now am I alone,' he thought. 'In all India is no one so alone as I . . . Who is Kim – Kim – Kim?' . . . He squatted in a corner of the clanging waiting-room; rapt from all thoughts; hands folded in lap and pupils contracted to pinpoints. In a minute – in another half-second – he felt he would arrive at the solution to the tremendous puzzle.

This is the Kim who is part of an India 'full of holy men stammering gospels in strange tongues', one of whom is the lama to whom he gives a free and unconditional love from which he never swerves; the Thibetan whose feet he kisses (though he is a Sahib) and to whom he puts himself in service as *chela*.

The scenes between Kim and the childlike holy man he serves are some of the most gently humorous in the book, and perhaps the tenderest in all Kipling: 'I had a fear,' the lama confesses, when he comes to find Kim at the school for which he is secretly paying the fees, 'that perhaps I came because I wished to see thee – misguided by the Red Mist of affection. It is not so . . .' 'But surely, Holy one,' Kim protests, 'thou hast not forgotten the Road and all that befell on it. Surely it was a little to see me that thou didst come.'

Service is a key word in *Kim*. In the world of this book a man can serve two masters; Kim does. That is the peculiar grace that Kipling finds for him – a capacity to be at once in two mind-spaces; one might go further and say, to achieve a reconciliation between the two worlds of India that Forster can only point to in the great final paragraph of his Indian book. If we believe in the achievement here it is because Kim himself sees no difficulty, so long as his soul is 'in order':

Roads were meant to be walked upon, houses to be lived in, cattle to be driven, fields to be tilled and men and women talked to. They were real and true – solidly planted on their feet – perfectly compre-hensible – clay of his clay, neither more nor less.

*

Roads. 'The Road and all that befell on it . . .'

As befits a work so 'nakedly picaresque', as Kipling calls it, roads, highways, destinations are essential to the book: the latter-day colonial arteries of the sub-continent – the Grand Trunk Road, the Track as it is called (the Railway) – and, closely related to both in the book's attempt to connect all the streams of Indian life and living, the Ganges (Mother Gunga), and the Way, the lama's lifelong search for his holy river. Committing oneself, for a time or a lifetime, to any one of them is to join the stream of life itself:

And truly, the Great Trunk Road is a wonderful spectacle. It runs straight, bearing without crowding India's traffic for fifteen hundred miles – such a river of life as exists nowhere else in the world . . . 'Now let us walk,' muttered the lama, and to the click of his rosary they walked in silence mile after mile. The lama, as usual, was deep in meditation but Kim's bright eyes were open.

This broad smiling river of life, he considered, was a vast improvement on the cramped and crowded streets of Lahore. There were new people and new sights at every stride – castes he knew and castes that were altogether out of his experience . . . It was beautiful to behold the many-yoked grain and cotton wagons crawling over the country roads; one could hear their axles complaining a mile away, coming nearer, till with shouts and yells and bad words they climbed up the steep incline and plunged on to the hard main road, carter reviling carter. It was equally beautiful to watch people, little clumps of red and blue and pink and white and saffron, turning aside to go to their own villages, dispersing and growing small by twos and threes across the local plain. Kim felt these things, though he could not give tongue to his feelings.

Kipling does of course. We can forgive a good deal of patriotism and steam for the moment, say, when Kim wakes and feels the whole sub-continent in motion and play about him:

The diamond-bright dawn woke men and crows and bullocks together. Kim sat up and yawned, shook himself, and thrilled with delight. This was seeing the world in real truth . . . India was awake, and Kim was in the middle of it, more awake and more excited than anyone, chewing on a twig that he would presently use as a tooth-brush; for he borrowed right-and-left-handedly from all the customs of the country he knew and loved.

There is more than a breath of the man himself in that, and a phrase Kipling uses of Kim might stand to describe how that free spirit works as the perfect embodiment of Kipling's writing self: 'Kim awaited the play of circumstances with an interested soul'; that is, in a state of readiness and expectancy before whatever was about to declare itself to him. Kipling repeats the idea in speaking, in the final chapter of *Something of Myself*, of the agency of writing itself. 'When your Daemon is in charge, do not try to think consciously. Drift, wait, and obey.'

That too, as Kim lives it and as Kipling at his most Kim-like acts it out, we might call 'the Great Game'.

Nation Review, *1978*
(revised and expanded, 2010)

MARCEL PROUST – THE BOOK

*I thought more modestly of my book and it would
be inaccurate even to say that I thought of those
who would read it as 'my' readers. For it seemed
to me that they would not be 'my' readers but
the reader of their own selves, my book being
merely a sort of magnifying glass like those
which the optician at Combray used to offer his
customers – it would be my book, but with its help
I would furnish them with the means of reading
what lay inside themselves. So that I should not
ask them to praise me or to censure me, but simply
to tell me whether 'it really is like that'.*

OF THE THREE GREAT writers who carry the novel
forward out of the nineteenth century and transform it in the light of the twentieth, it is Proust, for
all his elaborateness of style and the extensiveness of
his narrative, who seems most accessible to modern
readers. His work is a single unit. We have only to

enter the timeless dimension of Marcel's night-mind as it is opened to us on page one, to submit ourselves to the narrator's state of being, which is also a manner of speaking – a rhythm, a progression of cadences in which almost immediately the confession is made that 'it seemed to me that I myself was the immediate subject of my book' (of any book, that is, that he happens to be reading, but also the book he has begun to write) – and we are already set for a point, three thousand pages further on, when we shall at last know everything that was in the narrator's mind, and determined the rhythms of his thinking and feeling, when he set out. All the years and events of what is to be unfolded are contained in the timeless suspension of time with which the book opens; the great sad changes, discoveries, disappointments and losses to come are already there in the elegiac note it sounds, which is also the medium of their recovery. We have only to tune ourselves to the music and read on.

There is nothing here of that difficulty of interest that is provided, in Mann's case, by the unpredictable twists and turns of his writing between *Buddenbrooks* and *Doctor Faustus*, by the way the working life was refashioned by the life in time. Once Proust began on the definitive version of his great work, in 1909, he stopped time and insulated himself from events; his book was hermetically sealed. The coming of the war (not quite allowed for when it was conceived) required only a minor change of name (the substitution of Rheims for Chartres) to shift Combray far enough westward for the battle of Méséglise to wipe out the whole of Marcel's world.

The war did have an effect on the book, and a crucial one: by interrupting the publication of the second volume (which was already in proof) it allowed Proust to expand what he had written to three times its original length. But it did not push the novel in a new direction. The century's apocalyptic events were subsumed, incorporated into it, recognised as the necessary form of that sense of dissolution that is in the mood of the first sentence – another of those things the narrator did not yet know which is already, as so often in Proust, inherent in what is said. Where else but in wartime Paris, one wonders, could Charlus' sadistic and self-humiliating fantasies find their full expression – where except in Room 14b of Jupien's 'Temple of Shamelessness', where amidst talk of the heroism of the trenches, in real fear, during an air-raid, and at the hands of an off-duty serviceman, the Baron in his play-world is tied up and beaten? Where else but in a male brothel staffed by soldiers could a *Croix de Guerre* be lost and the narrator catch a last glimpse of that flower of French soldiery, and his own soiled embodiment of the aristocratic ideal, Count Robert Saint-Loup?

As for Joyce, whatever similarity we might find

between the reduction of epic time in *Finnegans Wake* to a single thunderclap and the telescoping of time in *A la Recherche* that makes the whole work, in some ways, a single breath (as it certainly would be if Proust could manage it, since containment, the holding of all things in a single moment of awareness, is his final purpose), the narrative methods of the two writers are essentially opposed; the similarities, even the uses of pastiche, are superficial.

The writing in Proust preserves a formal relationship between writer and reader that embodies the social conventions of a previous century – and not always even of the nineteenth.

Proust's digressions, elaborations, belle-lettrist set pieces, essaylike disquisitions and analyses belong to the nineteenth-century tradition of the *feuilleton*; his stance is that of the great memoir-writers. Complex as it is, this stance maintains, on the surface, a mannerly and confidential relationship between reader and narrator that embodies just that sense of formal intimacy, of private conversation, that occurs so often between the characters in the novel itself; in which things are revealed at leisure, and by subtle hints and evasions, and both sides are at all times aware that what is being told contains within it an element of falsity that belongs as much to seeing, telling, reading as to the falsity imposed by social conventions or to any conscious wish to deceive.

The manner, that is, involves a critique of the very narrative technique it employs, a twentieth-century scepticism of nineteenth-century 'realities' and of the novelistic style that embodies them. Proust too is a Modernist, though not in Joyce's way. Nothing could be further from Joyce's attempt to make the narrator disappear than Proust's use of the narrator's voice as the entire focus and justification of his book. Proust goes back, beyond Joyce or James, or even Flaubert, to a point where the voice of the writer is all we have, but makes his narrator not only an unreliable guide to the action but a puzzled and endlessly mistaken enquirer into what really occurred, even in situations where he was himself a major actor. The book is, in the end, about the power of language itself as an instrument of perceiving and knowing; but at no point does Proust allow it to break free, as Joyce does, into a world of its own. With great politeness it tells its own secret and sometimes contrary tale under the 'real' one. (Proust's Modernism too has its heirs. It is as if, along with Combray and so much else, the whole of contemporary French writing – I name only Barthes and Tournier – had opened like a flower out of that *tasse de thé*.)

It was also, of course, Proust's own unexpected flowering, this immense book-of-the-life.

Writing to his friend d'Albufera, in 1908, Proust names some of the projects that currently attract him.

un roman sur la noblesse
un essai sur Sainte-Beuve et Flaubert
un essai sur les Femmes
un essai sur la Péderastie (pas facile à publier)
une étude sur les vitraux
une étude sur les pierres tombales
une étude sur le roman

The list, which seems likely to distract the mind rather than focus it, is marvellously evocative for those of us who know, by hindsight, how many of those subjects were to find a place in the book Proust began in the following year. What astonishes us now is just the focus of that mind that allowed them all to be included and held; how, in a quite musical sense, the various themes must from the beginning have revealed themselves to him as being variations of one another.

The stages by which these separate works became *A la Recherche* are outlined very clearly by George Painter in Volume Two of his biography. Let me just remind readers of how important that 'essai sur Sainte-Beuve' was to be.

Proust had begun his novel yet again (*Jean Santeuil* can be seen as the first version of all) in February 1909. He had at the same time embarked on a series of parodies of great French writers, and it was out of these that he conceived the notion of *Contre Sainte-Beuve*. He abandoned the new version of the novel in

November for the essay, which was to take the form of a dialogue with his mother, in which he would discuss, each morning, what he was writing – a project that involved him in the resurrection of his mother and the whole of their life together, and led to an account of his sleeplessness, his night reading, and the occasion, long ago, when his mother had failed to give him his goodnight kiss – in fact, what we now recognise as the opening pages of *A la Recherche du Temps Perdu*. It was at this point, while he was engaged with Sainte-Beuve, that the business of the madeleine occurred (in reality a memory of the bit of tea-soaked toast he used to be given in his grandfather's garden at Auteuil), along with three other recollections that revealed to him the theory of 'involuntary memory'.

The Preface to *Sainte-Beuve*, without his having quite realised it, had become the opening chapter of *A la Recherche*. The novel was already underway. It had only to open out of itself in all its details. The process was one in which the interconnection of themes, and their metamorphosis into related or contrary forms, was essential to the creation of unity, and Wagner is mentioned often enough (obsessively, one might think) to make the term *leitmotif* relevant for at least one aspect of its extraordinary coherence. Proust's use of 'Wagnerian' techniques offers a significant clue to how we are to read him, both in detail and in depth, and to the way the whole book came into being.

The transexual theme, for example, is introduced quite early on, but in an exchange so fleeting, and so innocently placed, that we might miss it at first reading. (In Proust's case, one wants to say, the only possible *first* reading is the *second*.)

Two minor characters are involved, Sunday visitors at Combray: the Curé, who shares with the narrator a fascination with names that will itself account for many pages of the ensuing text, and one of his parishioners, Mlle Eulalie:

'Why yes, have you never noticed, in the corner of the window, a lady in a yellow robe? Well, that's Saint Hilaire, who is also known, you will remember, in certain parts of the country as Saint Illiers, Saint Hélier, and even, in the Jura, Saint Ylie. But these various corruptions of *Sanctus Hilarius* are by no means the most curious that have occurred in the names of the blessed. Take, for example, my good Eulalie, the case of your own patron, *Sancta Eulalia*; do you know what she has become in Burgundy? Saint Eloi, nothing more nor less! The lady has become a gentleman.'

This is on page 113 of Volume One in the Kilmartin translation. Quite soon after, in the description of Vinteuil's young daughter, the presence of the male within the female is hinted at again; and Mlle

Vinteuil is to become of course one of the book's many lesbians:

> His one and only passion was for his daughter, and she, with her somewhat boyish appearance, looked so robust that it was hard to restrain a smile when one saw the precautions her father used to take for her health . . . My grandmother had drawn our attention to the gentle, delicate, almost timid expression which might often be caught flitting across the freckled face of this otherwise stolid child. Whenever she spoke she heard her own words with the ears of those to whom she had addressed them, and became alarmed at the possibility of a misunderstanding, and one would see in clear outline, as though in a transparency, beneath the mannish face of the 'good sort' that she was, the finer features of a young woman in tears. (pp. 122–3)

It is part of the normal mode of the book that the narrator here is observing, and revealing, more than he at present knows; the language does it, and the attentive reader will not be surprised when the narrator witnesses, fifty pages later, the little scene between Mlle Vinteuil and her friend in which a homosexual relationship is presented openly, and in terms of humiliation and triumph that are themselves essential to the way Proust sees these things. The young narrator, without being aware of it, is being given clues (which he does not recognise) for solving the central puzzle of his own relationship, later, with Albertine; and it is in the early days of his fascination with her and the little band of girls at Balbec, on page 958 of this present edition, that the Eulalie/Eloi opposition recurs. It will solve for us, long before the narrator himself tumbles to it, the mystery of the 'little band' – though it is he, of course, who offers us the clue:

> So too when I ordered the cheese or salad sandwiches or sent out for the cakes which I would eat on the cliff with the girls, and which they 'might very well have taken turns to provide, if they hadn't been so close-fisted', declared Françoise, to whose aid there came at such moments a whole heritage of atavistic peasant rapacity and coarseness, and for whom one would have said that the divided soul of her late enemy Eulalie had been reincarnated, more becomingly than in St Eloi, in the charming bodies of my friends of the little band.

The link between Eulalie and the 'little band' belongs here to the character of Françoise, to her suspicion of both, and to her meanness; but the evocation of St Eloi in the prose, and that phrase 'the divided soul', already unties a knot. Our awareness of what is really going on in *A la Recherche* is always in the language the narrator uses rather than in what he consciously tells; and what is difficult to assess, because it changes from moment to moment, is whether the narrator's awareness belongs unconsciously to the dramatic moment or, as here perhaps, to the consciousness of hindsight in which he is recreating a past in the full knowledge at last of what it is.

This sort of play across the text, and under it, is one thing; but for most contemporary readers the game goes on well beyond it. In the feminised boys' names of the narrator's lovers – Gilberte, Albertine – and the transposition of males, as Proust himself put it in a conversation with Gide, 'à l'ombre des jeunes filles', a game is being played by the narrator (and this time I mean Proust himself) with the facts of his own life.

This of course is an impertinence – this reading outside the text into the life; but Proust's life, and its various transformations in the events of the novel, the equivocal placing of his narrator (another Marcel as we finally discover) halfway between historical fact and fiction, are as familiar now as the book itself, and too close to us for an awareness of them not to colour what we read. Proust anticipated this and took it into account. What we know of the life is part of the book, as a second reading is part of the first. It is as if, between dramatic present and recollected past, between what the narrator tells us and what the language reveals, between first and second reading, between the events of *A la Recherche* and the facts of

Proust's own life, we stood in the position described on page 114 by that same Curé who a page earlier has introduced, in his great innocence, the theme of a double sex. He is describing, this time, the view from the tower of St Hilaire:

'And then another thing; you can see at the same time places which you normally see one without the other, as, for instance, the course of the Vivonne and the irrigation ditches at Saint-Assise-lès-Combray, which are separated by a screen of tall trees, or again, the various canals at Jouy-le-Vicomte, which is *Gaudiacus vice comitis*, as of course you know. Each time I've been to Jouy I've seen a bit of canal in one place, and then I've turned a corner and seen another, but when I saw the second I could no longer see the first. I tried to put them together in my mind's eye; it was no good. But from the top of Saint-Hilaire it's quite another matter – a regular network in which the place is enclosed. Only you can't see any water; it's as though there were great clefts slicing up the town so neatly that it looks like a loaf of bread which still holds together after it has been cut up. To get it all quite perfect you would have to be in both places at once . . .'

To come specifically to that other 'double view', the created fiction and the life of the writer, we have, in a passage on Bergotte, Proust's own view of how we are to reconcile a writer's 'vices' with the high morality of his work – and I choose this aspect of the problem because it opens into a related one (Proust's presentation of the homosexual) that may itself be a stumbling-block to the modern reader. Proust is in no doubt that a contemporary writer's life will be known and is part of the text:

> Perhaps it is only in really vicious lives that the problem of morality can arise in all its disquieting strength. And to this problem the artist offers a solution in the terms not of his own personal life but of what is for him his true life, a general, a literary solution. As the great Doctors of the Church began often, while remaining good, by experiencing the sins of all mankind, out of which they drew their own personal sanctity, so great artists often, while being wicked, make use of their vices in order to arrive at a conception of the moral law that is binding upon us all. It is the vices (or merely the weaknesses and follies) of the circle in which they live, the meaningless conversation, the frivolous or shocking lives of their daughters, the infidelity of their wives, or their own misdeeds that writers have most often castigated in their books, without, however, thinking to alter their way of life or improve the tone of their household. But this contrast had never before been so striking as

it was in Bergotte's time, because, on the one hand, in proportion as society grew more corrupt, notions of morality became increasingly refined, and on the other hand the public became a great deal more conversant than it had ever been before with the private lives of literary men. (I, p. 601)

This passage may serve to excuse the contemporary reader from the charge of misreading or trivialising *A la Recherche* when he takes into account in his reading what he knows of the life; but it is meant, I think, in the light of what we do know, to excuse Proust himself from the charge of hypocrisy. Some of the events in the book that most shock us, as they also shock the narrator, are events in which Proust was personally involved. This is what so affronted Gide. Gide's diaries record two night conversations with Proust, on 13 May and 15 May 1921. They are worth quoting in full since they provide the context for his savage condemnation, when it appeared, of *Cities of the Plain*.

May 13, 1921

Far from denying his homosexuality he exhibits it, and I could almost say boasts of it. He claims never to have loved women save spiritually and never to have known love except with men.

May 15, 1921

We scarcely talked, this evening again, of anything but homosexuality. He says he blames himself for that 'indecision' which made him, in order to fill out the heterosexual part of his book, transpose *A l'ombre des jeunes filles* all the attractive, affectionate and charming elements contained in his homosexual recollections, so that for Sodom he is left nothing but the grotesque and the abject. But he shows himself very much concerned when I tell him that he seems to have wanted to stigmatise homosexuality; he protests; and eventually I understand that what we consider vile, an object of disgust, does not seem so repulsive to him.

Dec 2, 1921

I have read Proust's latest pages (Dec issue of NRF) with at first a shock of indignation. Knowing what he thinks, what he is, it is hard for me to see in them anything but a pretence, a desire to protect himself, a camouflage of the cleverest sort, for it can be to no one's advantage to denounce him. Even more: that offence to truth will probably please everybody; heterosexuals, whose prejudices it justifies and whose repugnances it flatters; and the others, who will take advantage of the alibi and their lack of resemblance to those he portrays.

Proust's attitude to homosexuality really is ambiguous, but Gide here seems over-sensitive. Despite its high moral tone, the long essay at the beginning of the *Cities of the Plain* (is this the 'essai sur la Pédérastie, pas facile à publier'?) can only be read as a piece of extended irony, in the typically French manner – going back to Jean Beyle and the Encyclopaedists – in which a straight-faced argument is destroyed by the conclusions it is pushed to and the absurdity, or comic inappropriateness, of the images with which it is embellished. Beginning and ending with the miraculous fertilisation of the orchid (which is after all natural, however improbable, and which the narrator misses only because he is so busy spying on Charlus and Jupien), it tends rather to mock the isolation of the Sodomites than to reinforce the standard view, equating their position, as so often in this text, with that of the Jews. It looks very much like a satirist's defence of what he is pretending to attack. Still, it is true that in the total design of the book, inversion (to use that quaint old term), both male and female, Sodom and Gomorrah, is one of the deeply corruptive elements of the world as the narrator perceives it. It is one of the book's great images of evil, part of its mythology; which is to say, perhaps, that Proust was more loyal to the structure of his book, which is also its morality, than to his own nature.

That is his choice as an artist, and he makes it, as the passage on Bergotte suggests, not only in defiance of the Mrs Grundys of this world but of the Gides as well. We accept the mythology because he imposes it so powerfully upon us in the reading; as we accept the old-fashioned notions of gender he makes use of because they obey so perfectly the demands of the work – its obsession with doubleness, ambiguity, travesty, metamorphosis, hermetic gesture and significance. They justify themselves by their adherence not to reality (books make their own reality) but to internal truth. Proust's psychology of homosexual behaviour (I do not mean his observation of it) belongs to myth. Modern readers will find little in *A la Recherche* to explain the nature of homosexuality or to further the cause of sexual politics, but Proust was neither a hypocrite nor a defector from the cause. He simply remained loyal to what he was creating rather than to what he was.

Given the vastness of the work – three thousand pages, a million and a quarter words – it is tempting to take the easy path and describe *A la Recherche* in terms of its 'set pieces': the business of the madeleine and the flowering of Combray and the whole world of the novel out of the cup of tea; the hawthorns of *Chez Swann*; the three men with the monocles, the morning sea at Balbec, the death of the narrator's grandmother, the courtship dance of Charlus and Jupien;

or, by taking four 'characters' in the La Bruyère sense, to see in it studies of the artist as writer (Bergotte), painter (Elstir), composer (Vinteuil) and actress (Berma); or to read it as an anthology of all the forms of passion – I mention only a few of the more obvious ways of working towards the centre of the book by choosing either characteristic details or one or more of its various 'structures'. But something ought to be said, however briefly, of the experience of the reading itself as its manifold views unfold before us, and of the whole as we see it at last from our many perspectives.

The narrator, at Combray, has two possible 'ways' of going – the Méséglise way that passes 'à côté du chez Swann', and what appears to be an alternative and opposite one, the Guermantes way. These constitute between them a divided topography of Combray and of the narrator's original world that becomes also a map of society and a map of the forces that move him this way and that within it.

Now it would be foolish to reduce to any simple scheme what in the writing, and in the reading, is so tangled and so full of qualification and nuance, but the narrator begins by exploring each of these ways in turn: Swann's way in the obsessive love which leads him to and then away from Gilberte and offers a preview of his own obsessive love for Albertine, and the other way which leads into society, into history, into that dream of ideal values – beauty, nobility – that is embodied for the narrator in the name of Guermantes. It is, of course, only at the very end of the book that the narrator discovers that his map was false, even in the topographical sense, since both ways can be taken to the same place.

But by the time the writer has seen this, and begun to reconstruct his view of things in accordance with 'truth', the place no longer exists, and each of its names has been given a significance outside him. Gilberte writes from Tansonville in *Time Regained*:

'Probably, like me, you did not imagine that obscure Roussainville and boring Méséglise . . . would ever be famous places. Well, my dear friend, they have become for ever a part of history, with the same claim to glory as Austerlitz or Valmy. The battle of Méséglise lasted for more than eight months; the Germans lost in it more than six hundred thousand men, they destroyed Méséglise, but they did not capture it. As for the short cut up the hill which you were fond of and which we used to call the hawthorn path, where you claim that as a small child you fell in love with me (whereas I assure you in all truthfulness it was I who was in love with you), I cannot tell you how important it has become. The huge field of corn upon which it emerges is the famous Hill 307, which you must have seen mentioned again and again in the bulletins . . .' (III, p. 778)

This final destruction of the world he knew, first the accuracy of his view of it, then the place itself, is where the narrator *begins*. His world is not resurrected; it is remade by a backward process and rediscovered at the point of the narrator's primal innocence and ignorance, so that he can once again describe it wrongly and make all its places famous in a different sense from the one Gilberte intended – famous because he creates them in all their details as they never were. The absolute destruction of Méséglise and all else, which seems so final and tragic as we are led towards it in the book, has already taken place before the writer creates it for us, and is the basis of its coming into its real existence. *That* is the demonstration of the power of memory but even more of the creative power of the word.

So too, if we take up another of the book's lines of development, the narrator's disillusionment – with the Guermantes and all they stand for, with love, with the whole innocent world of beginnings – that too has been accomplished before he enters into these things, in the work itself, with all the fullness and freshness of the enraptured child.

Innocence, Paradise, *can* be re-entered, but the process will lead again and again to inevitable expulsion.

It is worth stressing this double movement, forward and back, because it is easy to read *A la Recherche* only in terms of decline, as the destruction of innocence, the stripping of illusions, as a movement out of dreams into reality. That is certainly the traditional shape of the 'Bildungsroman'.

But Proust reverses the process. It is not in the end his acceptance of 'reality' that saves the narrator and justifies the long telling, but the power of those dreams themselves, the magic of naming, the super-reality of language itself, which can, in another form, restore and remake reality and in doing so proclaim the primacy of the act of memory and of mind.

This is an anti-realistic novel. Its end is always a new beginning. Its process is cyclic and its ultimate reality, as it exists both for writer and reader, is in the act of reading, of writing:

Experience had taught me only too well the impossibility of attaining in the real world to what lay deep within myself: I knew that Lost Time was not to be found again on the piazza of St Mark's any more than I had found it again on my second visit to Balbec or on my return to Tansonville . . . When I recapitulated the disappointments of my life as a lived life, disappointments which made me believe that its reality must reside elsewhere than in action, what I was doing was not merely to link different disappointments together in a purely fortuitous manner and in following the circumstances of my personal existence. I saw clearly that the disappointment of travel and the disappointment of love were not different disappointments at all but the varied aspects which are assumed, according to the particular circumstances which bring it into play, by our inherent powerlessness to realise ourselves in material enjoyment or in effective action. And thinking again of the extra-temporal joy which I had been made to feel by the sound of the spoon or the taste of the madeleine, I said to myself: 'Was this perhaps that happiness which the little phrase of the sonata promised to Swann and which he, because he was unable to find it in artistic creation, mistakenly assimilated to the pleasures of love, was this the happiness of which long ago I was given a presentiment – as something more supraterrestrial even than the mood evoked by the little phrase of the sonata – by the call, the mysterious, rubescent call of that septet which Swann was never privileged to hear, having died like so many others before the truth that was made for him had been revealed? A truth that in any case he could not have used, for though the phrase perhaps symbolised a call, it was incapable of creating new powers and making Swann the writer that he was not.' (III, p. 911)

Here finally, in coming to the heart of Swann's tragic failure, the narrator finds the truth about himself. He *does* have a task, since the 'truth that was made for him' has, by a kind of grace, been revealed to him in his own lifetime. He is a writer; his life is a book, and all the men and women he has encountered are characters in it.

The long process of this discovery, which is also the process through which the experience is to be remade, the coincidence of life and book, of feeling and seeing with telling, of the writer's experience being word for word and line for line the reader's, of its being *our* book, the book of our lives, all this is what constitutes not only the great achievement of *A la Recherche* (and it seems the ultimate and universal fiction – other novels are just novels) but also the great experience of reading it. Praise or censure, as Proust himself saw – and he was being modest – are neither here nor there, an irrelevance, when they are not merely a presumption. We discover in reading this book what it is to be a great writer. 'It really is like that.'

Scripsi, *1983*

PROUST'S *BELLES LETTRES*

THERE ARE WRITERS WHOSE letters we turn to in the assurance that what we will find there is what we find in all their work, the full creative self, since they cannot, whatever they are writing, be less than they are. Thomas Mann, in even the briefest request for information or reply to an enquiry, is always at full stretch, the instant representative of culture and mind: Isak Dinesen, in the letters she wrote from Africa between 1914 and 1931, had not yet found her vocation, but the voice is unmistakeable; we discover her as a writer before she has quite discovered herself. These writers intensely scrutinise; they argue, explore, give themselves up to playful speculation, produce, out of sheer exuberance and for the delight of their correspondents, observations on people, places, events, little passing phenomena, as if the mere taking up of a pen released in them that irresistible desire to exercise the spirit and entertain the world that is the writer's natural mode. No biographer can produce them for us as immediately or as richly as they produce themselves, and this because the production *is* immediate; we have to engage with them as their first readers did, in full spate, as agents vigorously on the move. To read such letters is to be *in medias res*, in life as it is being lived. We are too closely engaged to see what we are reading as 'secondary material'; as affording no more than clues, insufficient ones generally, to the other more composed sort of writing that is 'literature'.

The first thing to be said of Proust's letters is that we get very little of the writer in this mode: they are scarcely letters at all in the sense that Mann's are. As Proust himself points out (Vol. II, 136) they are 'correspondence', by-products of his social life, bread-and-butter letters – except that they are mostly jam: the man is hidden in them (in some cases it is their only purpose) behind a screen of art nouveau flourishes and circumlocutions, politenesses so artificial and perfunctory that they can scarcely be taken as the products of a 'writer' at all. The man who penned them is all poses. He watches himself; not analytically – not at all – and not to see what sort of figure he may be cutting among the immortals either, but out of fear of giving himself away. Wary always of nature, and of his own nature, he takes refuge in a kind of playfulness that is in contact with the truth only by lying at a tangent to it.

A good many of the letters are in code, some of them, like the ones to Reynaldo Hahn, in a form of baby talk or lovers' language (one thinks of the use of 'cattleyas' in *Du côté de chez Swann*) that may or may not go back to an actual affair – we simply cannot tell; nor can we make much sense of them. Others do speak a public language, but it is a language of effusive flattery and hyperbole that belongs so completely to the period, or to a particular class, or to the forms of French rhetoric, that it too is indecipherable now, and was perhaps, to the uninitiated, even then. What are we to do with all this if what we are interested in is sincerity and truth?

Proust is quite capable of writing plainly when the occasion demands, but for the most part it does not. Here he is (I, 92, May 1892) writing to Robert de Montesquiou. There is nothing indirect about this; nothing slavish either, considering that it is early enough in their acquaintance for Proust to be risking something, socially, by being so frank:

Dear Sir,

yesterday I did not answer the question you put to me about the Jews. For this very simple reason: though I am a Catholic like my father and brother, my mother is Jewish. I am sure you understand that this is reason enough for me to refrain from such discussions. I thought it more respectful to write this to you than to answer you in the presence of a third person. But I very much welcome this occasion to say something to you that I might never have thought of saying. For since our ideas differ, or rather, since I am not free to have the ideas I might otherwise have on the subject, you might, without meaning to, have wounded me in a discussion. I am not, it goes without saying, referring to any discussion that might take place between the two of us, for then I shall always take an interest in any ideas on social policy which you may choose to expound, even if I have a most fitting reason for not sharing them.

Yours,

Marcel Proust

He could also be robust in argument if he wanted. The reply he writes to the famous questionnaire from Maurice le Blond is wonderfully spirited, with all that combative and contrary play of mind that we might expect of these letters and so rarely get:

[About 27 or 28 August 1904]

Sir,

I have received the questionnaire you were good enough to send me. On the pretext of clarifying the meaning of the questions you pose, you hasten to point out the spirit in which the answer should be framed. And after two pages of highly interesting and as you say necessary explanations, you rightly consider the reader to be sufficiently 'prepared' so that you no longer need all that circumspection to express your thought and reveal your aim, which is not at all, is it, to 'conduct an inquiry', but to get a particular opinion endorsed. Thus after the 'necessary explanations' you give your questionnaire a new and entirely unequivocal form: 'Do you accept the *age-old tyranny* of Rome, etc.' 'Do you think the State has the right to *subjugate* artistic personality?' Faced with a question posed in this way, would anyone dare to reply that he is in favour of the tyranny of Rome or the subjugation of personality? . . .

And yet, Monsieur! Whether or not the State has 'the *right*' to subjugate artistic personality, do you think that so important since in no circumstances will it ever have the *power* to do so. What *can* subjugate the personality of an artist is, first of all, the beneficent force of a more powerful personality – and that is a servitude which is not far from being the beginning of liberty – and secondly, the pernicious effect of sloth, sickness or snobbery. But the 'State', Monsieur, how do you imagine the State can subjugate a personality?

Most of these letters are the product either of social tactics or private intrigue. There are, for example, the letters to older writers who might in some way be of use to him – Anatole France, Bergson, Sorel.

With an unctuousness and opportunism that would do credit to Bloch, whose exercises in shameless self-promotion provide some of the most savage humour in *A la Recherche du Temps Perdu*, they proceed in a sort of sideways style that involves a whole flurry of protective denials and negatives. The letter to Bergson is pure comedy:

25th May, 1904
Dear Sir,

Allow me to thank you with all my heart for your great kindness. You can imagine how much store I set by a few words from the philosopher I most admire, and how delighted I am at the thought that he might be prepared to say them. Had I not been so unwell recently I should simply have gone round to ask you whether you didn't find the whole thing excessive, and hence out of place, inopportune, perhaps ridiculous. If by any chance you did find it so, please don't take the trouble to write to me. I shall understand that your opinion was that it would be better to do nothing, on seeing that you have in fact done nothing. If on the other hand you find the idea natural and possible, don't bother to tell me either, and it will be a great joy to me, a just cause for gratitude and pride, that you should have done it.

Your most respectful admirer

Marcel Proust

That is the public side. On the other, the private side, Proust is forever urging his friends not to betray him to one another, or insisting that what he has just told one of them is 'tombe' – a tomb that must not be violated. Typical is his letter to Antoine Bibesco of September 1902. It is worth quoting at length, since as well as the usual accusations it makes reference to an early story, 'Fin de la jalousie' (the title is itself suggestive), in which there is already some question of the transposition of sexes. ('His Blue Eyes' here is Bertrand de Fénelon.)

My dear little Antoine,

Don't let what I am writing, which is very affectionate, make you angry (I'm not referring to 'doubts'; whether or not I have any has nothing to do with the case). But it horrifies me to have you ask me out loud whether I've asked Lauris if he thought 'His Blue Eyes' (not Lauris's blue eyes!) was nice or not so nice to me on a certain evening, etc.

Hadn't I made it absolutely clear that you were the *only* person to whom I had spoken of this business, that even Reynaldo doesn't know about it. Without stopping to think, you passed it on to others. I've done all I could to straighten things out. But if you're going to start dropping innuendoes to Lauris, etc.! Think of the impression it would make and what people would think of me. It's true that, especially at times like this when my 'Fin de la jalousie' is causing me mortal anguish, such childishness as what people will think of me seems unimportant. But it's not only on my account, I also owe it to my family not to let myself be taken for a Salaïst [homosexual]: gratuitously since I'm not one. Of course this wouldn't necessarily make me look like a Salaïst, but cut off from the interpretation which your knowledge of my character and of the daily course of events have given you, it would certainly look odd. Besides, my affectation of humility, etc etc. already makes me look servile enough, without adding to that impression by representing me to Lauris or others as living in expectation of a smile from the King. But the nub of the matter is that what the intensity of my sympathy for you, my absolute confidence in you, and my habit of telling you everything have made me confide in you, should remain privy to you and not be passed on to anyone whomsoever. Neither Lucien Daudet, nor Reynaldo, nor Yeatman, etc. know of it. So there is no reason to speak of it to Lauris, Billy or Constantin.

Of course none of this would be of the least interest if there had not been growing in the mind of the man who wrote these letters one of the supreme fictions of our century; if, submerged under all this fuss, there was not the great cathedral (his image) that by the end of the period covered by this second volume of letters had begun to rise, with all its towers and buttresses and elaborately sculptured figures, and figures behind figures, and was preparing to burst into the sun. It is for hints of the submerged cathedral that these letters draw us. They are there in plenty, but here too the eager student or lover of the book needs to take care.

Proust rejected the biographical approach, and not only because he had so much, in his own case, to fear from it. In simply being what it is, *A la Recherche*, with its paradoxical and contradictory view of things – of events, characters, even geography – its misapprehensions, provisions, corrections, recorrections, revelations that make a kind of nonsense, but only a kind of nonsense, of what has gone before, is a direct assault on that method and should itself warn us against bringing these letters, or any known 'facts' of Proust's life, to a reading of his book.

There is always a gap between the observable life of an artist and his creations. The wider it appears (think of Mozart) the more we are led to wonder what hidden and unknowable *other life* there must have been in the man that could produce works so much larger than his known self could encompass; what leap of being must have occurred in him that nothing in the apparent life accounts for. The gap is larger in some artists than in others. In Proust it is very large indeed. Literary detectives and biographers, for all the facts and witnesses they may call on, are given very little foothold and have a long way to fall.

We see the problem in Gide's rejection of *Du côté de chez Swann*. The trivial person he knew could not have written a great novel so the novel he was reading was not great. Proust was to have the same problem himself with Cocteau.

One way of putting it is this: there is, as we have seen, a good deal of Bloch in Proust, as there was a good deal of Charlus, but Bloch could not have written *A la Recherche*; and neither could Proust if there had not been enough of Bloch in him, and of Charlus too, for him to see these characters from the inside as well as observing them satirically from a distance.

Take these two letters of 1908, the first to an old school-friend, de Lauris, who has broken a leg in a motor accident, the second to a young man he scarcely knew, the Vicomte de Pâris. They are, it seems to me, in the style of Charlus, as the letter to Bergson was in the style of Bloch:

Wed, 7th (?), October 1908
At the moment I'm unable to leave my bed, but I hope to come and see you soon. It is always delightful to

see you, but even more gratifying now: each of your limbs so miraculously spared, your beautiful, gentle hands which from time to time, when I express a doubt about your friendship, seek mine in a gesture of persuasive eloquence, your whole body whose natural gait, immobilised now but not altered, is the only one I know that is entirely devoid of conventional mannerisms, swift in its movement towards what it desires or knows itself to be desired by, and above all your eyes, which darken so quickly if a sadness traverses your heart but in the depths of which, in an instantaneous effulgence, magnificent azure flashes pierce the clouds – your whole body, indeed, is what I should like to see and touch now after having too long forgotten that it is the necessary condition of all that spiritual spontaneity which is *you* and which we love and for which we must worship the integrity of this symbol of yourself, this body in which your spirit dwells, those hands through which the force of your grasp runs as through a unique and highly conductive metal . . . It seems to me that I have too exclusively loved your mind and your heart hitherto and that now I would experience a pure and exalting joy, like the Christian who eats the bread and drinks the wine and sings *Venite adoremus*, in reciting in your presence the litany of your ankles and the praises of your wrists.

Alas, people have always been so cruel and uncomprehending about me, that these are things which I

scarcely dare to say, because of the misunderstandings and misinterpretations which would spring up
in others' thoughts. But you who know me and grasp
with your infallible intelligence the palpable reality
of what I am, will understand how purely moral and
reverently paternal is what I say to you.

Friday evening, 12 June

It would be easy for me – and you have been unfriendly
to me for some time – to leave you with the notion
which pleases you, and which is a matter of indifference to me, as to this evening's little incident. But I
have such a sad proof to give you of the sincerity of
what I said and the stupidity of what you thought, or
claimed to think, that I cannot resist the melancholy
pleasure of indulging in these memories. My poor
Mama whom I lost nearly three years ago – without
your ever having offered a single word of sympathy
for a misfortune so great that you would have taken
pity if you had the least suspicion of it – my poor
Mama thought you had the most handsome face of
any man she knew, and she knew that I also admired
your looks. If you pretended to find something funny
in the way I told you this, it's because I didn't want to
embarrass you with a compliment *coming from me*
in front of Madame de Chimay. And after you left
us, I told Madame de Chimay that mama used to say
to me: 'I find M. de Pâris much better-looking than

Lucien Daudet.' This you must not repeat because he's a friend whom I'm fond of and who was very fond of Mama. But I told the Princesse de Chimay because *she* knew very well that I would never link Mama's memory with anything that wasn't *the very truth itself* . . . I would never profane the memory of the person I loved more than anything in the world, in order to pay you a compliment or relieve you of the bitterness of an alleged criticism, which in any case I wouldn't mind the least. You are not worth my having tired myself writing you all this. But the truth is worth it.

The two occasions are different of course. De Lauris is an intimate, quite accustomed, one might guess, to these passionate outpourings, which as we see here, even allowing for a certain degree of literariness and working up, can be pretty strong. Even so, having made the advance, Proust finds it necessary, once he sees what he is saying – once he sees, that is, how others may see it – to beat a retreat. But the de Pâris incident was seriously embarrassing; we may judge the nature of it from the letter to de Lauris. Proust attacks the recipient of his compliment, his favours; sets *him* at fault, insists that he has been misinterpreted, acts wounded, and punishes the young man for a crime he may not even know he has committed. He was to make brilliant use of that sort of ploy when he came to Charlus.

And the emerging outline of the book itself?

One can see clearly enough the points in time at which the potential of the thing begins to become clear. It's like those picture-puzzles whose points we used to join up as children to produce at last an aeroplane or a jaunty automobile or Mickey Mouse. It was miraculous. At one moment nothing was to be seen, then suddenly, in the next, there it was.

Some of those points are: the Preface to Proust's translation of *Sesame and Lilies* ('Sur la lecture') which is in fact a first draft of the opening pages of the book; the death of his mother in September 1905; his reappearance, after a long period of mourning, at a musical soirée at the Princesse de Polignac's in 1907, when he notes how people he used to know have aged; his first adult visit, in August of that year, to Cabourg (the Balbec of *A la Recherche*), where he visited the painter Vuillard and hired a series of chauffeur-driven cars from the Taximetres Unic de Monaco; then, in a letter of May 6, 1908 to his friend d'Albufera, the list of projects he has in mind: 'a study on the nobility / a Parisian novel / an essay on Sainte-Beuve and Flaubert / an essay on Women / an essay on Pederasty (not easy to publish) / a study of stained-glass windows / a study of tombstones / a study on the novel.' Then in mid-December 1908 in a letter to Mme de Noailles: 'Will you allow me without preamble to ask your advice. I should like, although I'm very ill, to write a study of

Sainte-Beuve. The idea has taken shape in my mind in two different ways between which I must choose; but I have neither the will-power nor the clearsightedness to do so. The first would be a classical essay . . . the second begins with an account of a morning, my waking up and Mama coming to my bedside; I tell her I have an idea for a study of Sainte-Beuve; I submit it to her and develop it. Can you tell me which of them seems the better.'

By May 1909 he is asking de Lauris about 'Guermantes' ('which must have been the name of some people as well as a place'), insisting in his next letter: 'No, Georges, I am not writing a novel.' By the next month, what he still refers to as 'Sainte-Beuve' ('I'm hard at work on it though the results are execrable') has already become the first draft of *A la Recherche*, and by mid-August he is offering it to a publisher, Vallette: 'I am finishing a book which in spite of its provisional title, *Contre Sainte-Beuve, souvenir d'une matinée*, is a genuine novel and an extremely indecent one in places. One of the principal characters is a homosexual . . . Perhaps, before giving me a definitive answer, you would like to have a sample of this production. I could in a few days have the first hundred pages copied for you very legibly, or even typed. But they are of the greatest purity. If the thought of the others frightens you and you would like to be reassured on the point (there isn't a hint of *pornography*) I can have a few passages copied for you but the text is not absolutely definitive.'

Knowing what we do of Proust's methods, and how the novel was to expand over the next decade and more, that last admission may raise a smile, but the point is that the first version of the book was already done.

Of course it was not done, and never would be; it was a work that was to remain open till the very last to every sort of contingency. To the explosive effect of his developing relationship with the young chauffeur Agostinelli, who has been on the scene as early as August 1907, driving Proust round Normandy 'like a cannonball' while they looked at cathedrals, but as no more at that point than a charming servant; the equally explosive effects of the War.

All that was still to come. What we see in these present letters, or rather do not see, is the crystallisation in Proust's mind of all those diverse elements of his interest that, in a series of flashes we can only imagine, were to coalesce and take shape as a new substance altogether. It is a process any writer will recognise, but one that can never, while it is happening, be analysed, or later reconstructed: a sense, the moment a new work begins to seed, of the whole universe attending, taking an interest, turning itself as it were in the book's direction, so that everything one comes across – in the daily papers, in the street, in what begins to come up out of the depths of memory – out of the depths too of an experience one may not yet have had – immediately finds a place there, in indissoluble connection. Proust tells us, and his correspondents, nothing of this, but that it was happening – that the points were beginning to connect – is undeniable in what suddenly, miraculously, appears. It was a process that was to go on till the very end; and we hear nothing of that, either.

My own guess is that the key date for Proust was Tuesday, September 26, 1905, the day his mother died.

He was a devoted son. Filial piety is a kind of religion with him. He never misses an opportunity here to write to a friend who has lost a parent – there are at least a dozen such letters; he even wrote to people he hardly knew, like Henry van Blarenbergh. His most passionate outburst in these volumes is over a novel whose author, Paul Léautaud, had committed the sin of treating family feeling with cynicism:

> But M. Léautaud's *Amours*! I won't speak of the book's moral baseness, because I should be incapable of doing so. I don't know any words that could express the pain I felt on seeing a human being feign sentiments beside which those of the cruellest murderer would be estimable . . .

The phrase 'the cruellest murderer' sits oddly here when we recall Proust's extraordinary essay 'Sentiments filiaux d'un parricide' (an ambiguous enough title) that he must have written in the same month, January 1907. The piece appeared in *Figaro* on February 1st.

Henry van Blarenbergh, recipient of one of those famous letters of condolence on the death of his father, had stabbed his mother to death, then shot himself. Proust, in writing of the affair, raises what might have seemed, as he put it, a matter of mere 'blood and madness' to a point where it can be likened to 'one of the Greek dramas, the performance of which was almost a sacred ceremony'. It ends with a paragraph that was cut by a sub-editor. We know this from an exchange here with Gaston Calmette, the editor of *Figaro*, in which Proust quotes the passage:

> 'Let us remember that for the ancients there was no altar more sacred, surrounded with more profound superstition and veneration, betokening more grandeur and glory for the land that possessed them and had dearly disputed them, than the tomb of Oedipus, at Colonus, and the tomb of Orestes at Sparta, that same Orestes whom the Furies had pursued to the feet of Apollo himself and Athene, saying: "We drive from the altar the parricidal son."'

The death of his mother was sacred to Proust, there is no doubt of that, but the sacred for him had its terrible side, and he must have known, obscurely, and perhaps even consciously, that he could only come into full possession of his life, and of his work too, when she was gone; partly because certain aspects of his nature had to be hidden so long as she was there to be a witness of them, as we see in the emergence in his later letters of the Charlus in him, but also because, to become the centre about which he can begin to compose his book, she had to move into the most active part of his soul, into memory. Part of his horror of losing her, one feels – how large a part we can only guess – was the terror of what he would have, eventually, to *do*. Only he can have known at this point what this might be, and how the elements of the great possibility were more and more pushing him towards an act of final dedication and withdrawal.

This second volume ends, very fittingly, with the work that was done at last to insulate him from the flushing of his neighbour's cistern and all the 'noise of the Boulevard, between Printemps and Saint Augustin'.

This was in the apartment in his uncle's house, 102 Boulevard Haussmann, which he subrented. The old apartment in the Rue de Courcelles, which he shared with his mother, like the family house at Illiers, was free now to enter the more fruitful realm of 'time past', of recall, and some of its furniture, as we see here in a letter to Mme Catusse, went into a depository, to be presented later (another odd note in the history of Proust's filial piety) to the male brothel he helped finance for 'Jupien'.

Writing to Antoine Bibesco in July 1904, Proust says: 'I've described my life since your departure exclusively in frivolous terms but you are well aware of course that *"this is the apparent life"* and that *"the real life is underneath all this"*.' (He is quoting from Ruskin and in English.)

These letters belong to the apparent life, but it is what is underneath that matters. The 'apparent Proust' we already know only too well, as a snob, a dilettante, a neurotic invalid, social butterfly, fusspot, closet 'Salaïst' or practiser of 'Josephism'. What is not so well known is what a kind and considerate man he was (see the letters here to Mme Strauss), and how generous he could be:

> Too ill to reply to anything in your letter, to which I've so much to reply. But I wanted to write to you simply to say this trivial thing: You say that your prize gave you pleasure only because of the thirty louis. Do you then need money at the moment? As you know, I now alas have my little fortune at my own disposal. It isn't very large since I can't keep the only thing in the world I care about, the flat in which I've lived with Mama these last few years. But thank heavens it would enable me to put whatever you wanted at your disposal, if you had the least need of money. And with what pleasure. Don't tire yourself answering me. Just a figure, if you want anything. (To Robert Dreyfus, around 25 June 1906)

But there is also his larger and deeper compassion.

After all the bitterness of the Dreyfus affair, whose shadow still hangs over these letters, and with the full account of it, in his case, still to come, he is able to write to Mme de Noailles of General Mercier's appearance before the assembly on July 13, 1906:

> In spite of my great pity for General Mercier he's an out-and-out scoundrel . . . All the same, when I think that I organised the first list in *L'Aurore* to demand a revision, and that so many politicians who were then wild anti-Dreyfusards now mortally insult on the floor of the House this old man of seventy-five who was courageous enough to appear, surrounded by a hostile pack, with nothing to say, knowing that he would have no argument to put forward except that the procedure (of the Court of Appeal!) had been *irregular, illegal,* and *in camera*! . . . It's horrible to read, for even in the wickedest man there's a poor innocent horse toiling away, with a heart, a liver and arteries in which there's no malice, and which suffer.

This points more clearly than the long parade of characters in these letters who might be 'sources', to what made *A la Recherche* possible, to what it was in the 'apparent' writer of these letters that was preparing 'underneath'.

Scripsi, *1989*

KAFKA

I CAN THINK OF no twentieth-century writer, not even Proust, who works so close to the facts of his own life as Kafka; the facts, that is, of his inner life. As he put it in *Letter to the Father* in November 1919, 'My writing was all about you; all I did there, after all, was to bemoan what I could not bemoan upon your breast . . . But how little all that amounted to! It is only worth talking about at all because it has happened in my life.'

That life was over in 1924. Kafka was forty-one. But the works he left, the two unfinished novels, *The Castle* and *The Trial*, such stories as 'In the Penal Colony', 'Before the Law', 'The Burrow', seem at this distance among the most personal responses we have to what happened in Europe in the two decades that followed his death: the development of opposing but related ideologies into murderous dictatorships of

Left and Right, each with its own fanatical adherents, its departments of exemplary punishment under the Law, its secret police, informers, show trials, camps of correction, camps of extermination. In 1943–44 all three of Kafka's sisters and their families disappeared into one or another of the killing machines of the Third Reich. Was Kafka unusually prescient?

His own explanation is altogether simpler. He had merely, as he tells us – but to an intense degree – absorbed 'the negative aspects of his own time'; by applying himself, with the forensic skill and meticulous attention to detail of the trained insider, to the world immediately around him: to its banalities, but also to what was comic and perverse and sinister and even monstrous in it, working outwards from his family and from the vantage point of a provincial capital of the highly bureaucratised Kaiserlich and Königlich Austro-Hungarian Empire of which he was himself an assiduous functionary.

So many of the facts of Kafka's life read like unlikely happenings from the stories. When the vast institution of the Empire collapsed at last in November 1918, after a humiliating defeat in the First World War and under the pressure for independence of its subject nations, a medal was on its way to Kafka for his years of dedicated service to a now vanished Emperor.

*

The Kafkas were Czechs but German-speaking. After a brief period in the family business (his father Herman, the son of a country butcher from Southern Bohemia, was the owner of a large clothing warehouse on the outskirts of Prague), Kafka worked for a time in a legal office, served a year as intern in the law courts, then for fourteen years, from 1908 until his retirement in 1922 when he was already dying of tuberculosis, was an official of the semi-governmental Workers' Accident Institute, for which he wrote three important reports: *Mandatory Insurance in the Construction Industry* and *Measures to Prevent Accidents (in Factories and Farms)*, 1908, and *Workers' Accidents and Insurance Management*, 1911 – titles that might go unremarked alongside 'Report to an Academy' and 'Investigations of a Dog' among the stories, and share with 'The Burrow' ('Der Bau') a meticulous concern with the minutiae of construction (*Bau*) and the many precautions that must be taken in the cause of insurance and safety. A good deal of what Kafka was occupied with at his place of work gets carried over, in a parodic way, into the stories, and the 'office style' that was in force there determines their tone, the disturbing dryness with which even the most appalling situation is presented as simply one of many variations on the normal; as in what is perhaps the best known of his stories, 'Die Verwandlung' of 1912, whose German title, with its native derivation, is plainer, more homely and down-to-earth than the one we know it by, 'The Metamorphosis'.

The members of a Prague family wake one morning in their comfortable apartment to find that their son and brother, a commercial traveller, in accordance with the body's unpredictable laws of transformation, either in developing the symptoms of a disease (tuberculosis for example, or elephantiasis, or multiple sclerosis), or, in the psychosomatic manner proposed by such psychoanalysts as Freud, Georg Groddeck or the William Stekel of *Onanism and Neurosis* or *Sadism and Masochism*, has in a single night assumed the form – hard carapace, several thin legs like feelers – of a giant cockshafer or beetle. The story's originality lies less in the fantastic nature of its events than in the attitude Gregor Samsa takes to his new condition and his family's determination to treat it as a misfortune like any other; to be accepted, and quietly come to terms with, like any other of life's unhappy vicissitudes.

Kafka was never, like his contemporaries Heinrich and Thomas Mann, Musil, Hermann Broch, Stefan Zweig, a full-time professional writer. But from 1909 onwards he published regularly in newspapers and periodicals – some local, some within the wider German-speaking world – and between 1913 and 1924 printed five collections of his longer stories; a sixth, *The Hunger Artist*, went to the printers at the end of 1923 and was published in the *Prager Presse* on April 20, six weeks after his death.

These are the works that Kafka refers to in the note he left for his friend Max Brod, who was to be his literary executor: 'Of all my writings, the only books that can stand are these: *The Judgement*, *The Stoker*, *Metamorphosis*, *Penal Colony*, *Country Doctor* and the story "The Hunger Artist".' If we except 'The Burrow', 'The Great Wall of China' and 'Investigations of a Dog', which are only technically unfinished, and the three novels, also unfinished, this constitutes all his major works of fiction. It was the novels, *America*, *The Trial* and *The Castle*, that he directed Brod to destroy.

What this suggests is an ambitious and hard-working writer, deeply embedded in the dailiness of living and in his own culture and times. For all his private difficulties, he was neither isolated nor unrecognised. In close contact with other writers, widely read in all branches of German literature, he goes to lectures and public readings by visiting authors and critics, admires Dickens, goes to the movies and laughs; sees Wedekind's *Erdgeist* ('Lulu') and finds it 'clear, even in retrospect, so that one goes home peaceful and aware of oneself'; refreshes himself again and again, as Mann does, with the clarity and cheerfulness of Goethe; reads Lenz 'incessantly – such is my state – he restores me to my senses'; discovers, in the midst of his own engagement difficulties, Kierkegaard, and finds 'As I suspected, his case, despite the essential differences, is very similar to mine'; notes in his diary, 'Afternoon at Werfel's with Max Pick, read In the Penal Colony aloud, am not entirely dissatisfied except for its glaring faults . . . Werfel read some poems.'

Two insights into the decisions he made as a writer are worth a closer look.

One is from a diary entry of January 1912:

It is easy to recognise in me a concentration of all my forces in writing. When it became clear to my organism that writing was the most productive direction for my being to take, everything rushed in that direction and left me empty of all those activities which were directed towards joys of sex, eating, drinking, philosophical reflections, and above all music. Naturally I did not find this purpose independently and consciously, it found itself.

It was late in the same year, on the night of September 22–23, that he wrote, in a single burst, 'The Judgement', the first story in which he felt his powers were fully expressed.

The other is the second part of his posthumous directive to Brod:

When I say that these five books may stand, I do not mean that I wish them to be reprinted and handed down to posterity. On the contrary, should they disappear altogether that would please me best. Only since they do exist, I do not wish to hinder anyone who might want to, from keeping them.

This sort of equivocation, this giving with one hand and taking back with the other, is typical. Kafka is forever torn between self-expression – self-display – and self-abnegation; the wish to put himself forward and assert his existence, to make his presence felt, and the wish to 'disappear'; between 'singing', like the heroine of 'Josephine the Singer, or the Mouse Folk' (in his case, reading his stories aloud), or performing on the variety stage like the Ape of 'Report to an Academy' – and silence.

The urge to perform as a writer is as existentially necessary to him as singing is to Josephine, even if, as in her case, it is only 'the usual squeaking'. It can be altruistic (Josephine's singing somehow protects her endangered mouse folk) but is nonetheless in both senses 'vain'. Firstly because it is open to the charge of self-indulgence; secondly because it leads nowhere, that is, 'falls on deaf ears'. Then there is the case of the Hunger Artist whose equivalent of writing or singing is rigorously to abstain from food, which, however spectacular it may be as a public performance, has no existential justification at all. As he confesses on his deathbed, he starves himself 'because I couldn't find the food I liked. If I had found it, believe me, I should have made no fuss and stuffed myself like you or anyone else.' When the Hunger Artist is replaced in his cage, it is by a panther, a creature who behaves 'naturally', and does not starve himself, or sing like Josephine, or learn, like the Ape, to mimic humans, or justify his existence, as Kafka does, by writing, and he does not miss his freedom, either – that freedom that the Ape tells us was 'not to be her choice', because in the panther's case 'his noble body, furnished almost to the bursting point with all it needed, seemed to carry freedom around with it too'.

For Kafka, the context for all these questions – freedom, spiritual nourishment, existential self-expression and fulfilment in writing – was the family.

There was the expectation, for example, that he should marry and become a father himself. Marrying, as he puts it, 'founding a family, accepting all the children that come [is] the utmost a human being can succeed in doing'. His engagement to Felice Bauer, and the correspondence between them, makes up one part of the story, as does his second engagement, also broken, to Julie Wohryzek; and Kafka did in fact father a son: to one of Felice Bauer's friends, Grete Bloch, though he never knew it. (The boy died, aged seven, in 1921; Bloch was murdered by a Nazi soldier in 1944.) But Kafka's deepest engagement was with his father.

'The Judgement', the first of the finished stories with which he was genuinely pleased, deals with a low-key quarrel between father and son that ends in the son's accepting the sentence of death his father has casually delivered, by rushing out of the house and drowning himself in the river below – the earliest dramatisation of a range of anxieties and obsessions that Kafka would explore more fully elsewhere: guilt before some unspecified but irresistible law; a court that is tyrannical but whose terms cannot be questioned; shame, self-immolation as an act of spiritual self-justification. But the son's disproportionate reaction, and the story's appeal not to psychology but to some more impersonal agency or force, leaves its meanings unclear. What it refers back to in Kafka's own situation finds its clearest expression seven years later in the *Letter*, where the Father appears as a distant and unresponsive but undeniable stand-in for God.

*

The Kafkas, father and son, were often in bitter disagreement. As an assimilated Jew, Herman Kafka was scathing, for example, of his son's preoccupation with Jewishness. As early as 1911 Kafka writes in the diaries of 'the Jewish question' and its solution; of the 'transitional state', as he puts it, of European Jewry, whose end is at that point 'unpredictable'.

When, six months later, a troupe of Yiddish actors sets up in a Prague café, Kafka becomes one of their regular patrons (he speaks of a dozen plays), and his father warns him, 'Whoever lies down with dogs gets up with fleas,' a phrase Kafka never forgives, and which he refers to eight years later, in the *Letter*. Meanwhile Kafka turned to Jewish history, Talmudic studies, Jewish literature, and in December 1911 writes admiringly of such small national literatures as Yiddish and Czech, describing them as 'the keeping of a diary by a nation, which is entirely different from historiography, and results in a more rapid (and yet always closely scrutinised) development', though he thinks of himself as belonging to a larger one, German, and within that as being quite unconnected to its Jewish strand. As late as 1922 he distinguishes his particular tone and style from the kind of ingratiating appeal to an audience that the anti-semitic Hans Blüher identifies, in his *Secessio Judaica*, as unmistakeably 'Jewish'.

The immediate occasion of *Letter to the Father* was the failure, in November 1919, of Kafka's last attempt to marry, which becomes, in the writing, his final effort to justify himself to the one judge whose approval he wants but who will never, he knows, grant it to him. Within the sphere of family theology it is also, and more importantly, Kafka's definitive attempt to vindicate himself to the author of his existence:

> For me as a child, everything you shouted at me was positively a heavenly commandment. I never forgot it, it remained for me the most important means of forming a judgement of the world, above all of forming a judgement of yourself. And there you failed entirely. Since as a child I was together with you chiefly at meals, your teaching was to a large extent about proper behaviour at table. What was brought to the table had to be eaten up, there could be no discussion of the goodness of the food – but you yourself often found the food uneatable, called it 'this swill', said 'that brute' (the cook) had ruined it . . . Please understand me rightly, these would in themselves have been utterly insignificant details, they only became depressing for me because you, the man who was so tremendously the measure of all things to me, yourself did not keep the commandments you imposed on me.

The arbitrariness of the laws, the injustice of their imposition, opens up for the child here a vision both of the divine law and the laws of the state. The result is a formulation that anticipates, as more than one commentator has observed, the racial laws of two decades later, from which there was no escape because the crime had been created to fit the man: guilt was a question not of doing but of being. 'The world,' as Kafka puts it, 'was divided for me into two parts . . . one in which I, the slave, lived under laws that had been invented only for me, and which I could, I did not know why, never completely comply with; then a second world, which was infinitely remote from mine, in which you lived, concerned only with government, with the issuing only of orders and with annoyance at their not being observed.'

Readers of Kafka will immediately recognise here the situation of K in *The Trial*, but also that of the old man in 'Before the Law'. What might also be recognisable is the spiritual state of the Kafkian hero, which, since it has its grounds in inequality of power, is also a political one: 'I was continually in disgrace. Either I obeyed your orders, and that was a disgrace, since they applied after all only to me, or I was defiant, and that was a disgrace too, for how could I presume to defy you; or I could not obey, for instance, because I had not your strength, your appetite, your skill, in spite of which you expected it of me as a matter of course; this was the greatest disgrace of all. What moved me in this way was not the child's reflections but his feelings.'

That last sentence is important because it relates not simply to the means by which Kafka understood his predicament but to what he was led by when he reproduced it, in so many forms, in his writing.

It was, for example, by drawing on his own obsession with punishment, his own self-destructive need to make the realisation of guilt coincident with the moment of execution, that he was able to create, in 'In the Penal Colony', a situation that dramatises from both sides, that of executioner and victim, the punishment camps of a later decade. As it was through his own fanatical attachment to the source of tyrannical power, the father, that he is able to conceive, in the young officer of the story who climbs into his own death-machine, the most convincing image we have in fiction of the dedicated Nazi.

Kafka knew all about these emerging types of his own generation, whose lives would fulfil themselves in a future he would not live to see, because he had already discovered in himself what they embodied of the 'negative aspect' of the time.

As for the coming tyranny, the following passage is not, as we might imagine, a premonition of the Führer's table-talk at Berchtesgaden but another evocation of the paterfamilias of Prague:

From your armchair you ruled the world. Your opinion was correct, every other was mad, wild, *meschugge*, not normal . . . You were capable, for instance, of running down the Czechs, and then the Germans, and then the Jews, and what is more not only selectively but in every respect, and finally nobody was left but yourself. For me you took on the enigmatic quality that all tyrants have whose rights are based on their person, not on reason.

Speaking towards the end of the *Letter* of what writing meant to him, he says:

I have already indicated that in writing and in what is connected with it, I have made some attempts to escape, with the very smallest of success; they will scarcely lead any farther; much confirms this for me. Nevertheless it is my duty to watch over them, or rather, my life consists in this, letting no danger that I can avert, indeed no possibility of such a danger, approach them. Marriage is the possibility of such a danger, admittedly also the possibility of the greatest advancement; for me however it is enough that it is a possibility of danger!

Writing was the one area in which he could declare his independence. What he meant by that, and what he sacrificed to achieve it, is clear from an earlier passage:

If I want to become independent in the particular unhappy relationship in which I stand to you, I must do something that will, if possible, have no relation to you at all; marrying is, it is true, the greatest thing of all and provides the most honourable independence, but it is at the same time in the closest relationship to you . . . Precisely this close relation does lure me towards marrying. I picture the equality that would arise between us, and which you would be able to understand better than any form of equality, as so beautiful precisely because I could then be a free, grateful, guiltless, upright son, and you could be an untroubled, untyrannical, sympathetic, contented father. But to this end it would be necessary to make all that has happened as though it never happened, which means we ourselves would have to be cancelled out. Being what we are, marrying is barred to me through the fact that it is precisely and peculiarly your most intimate domain.

The painful irony here is that the real cancelling out, the refusal to propagate, the destruction of the line, is accepted in favour of the moral cancelling out of one's own experience. But this acceptance of extinction in *fact*, while asserting the continuance of moral and spiritual existence, is exactly what Kafka is all about. It is like the end of *The Trial*, where Josef K dies 'like a dog'. '"Like a dog!" he said,' and then, as that famous sentence goes on, 'it was as if he meant the shame of it to outlive him'.

That shame, both for himself as victim and for his executioners, is the small assertion of identity, of having once been alive and present, that survives for Kafka as the expression of a fate, an individual existence and end, that has been willingly embraced.

Few of the stories reach this point. But the dry precision of Kafka's narrative, unlike the baroque playfulness of later fabulists, is itself an acceptance of fate. The circumstances may be repeatable and therefore ordinary, but they are made extraordinary by being accepted (claimed) by the protagonist as uniquely his. Fate as Kafka reveals it is a series of events in which the end is determined the moment the various Ks of the novels or stories accept that this, and this only, is the life, the story they are in.

The hypersensitive canine in 'Investigations of a Dog', one of the last of these stories (summer 1922), is concerned, like his creator, with ultimate questions: canine nature, the earth and the sources within it of 'nurture', the 'incantations' that are associated with nurture, and, as the canine puts it, a question that is especially close to Kafka, 'How long will you be able to endure the fact that the world of dogs, as your researches make more and more evident, is pledged to silence and always will be?'

This dog, like the Hunger Artist, devotes himself to fasting, but unlike the Hunger Artist he does it in good faith, since, though in the canine world fasting is forbidden, he believes that 'the highest effort among us is voluntary starving'.

Close to death from hunger, he is visited by a beautiful hound, a hunting dog who insists that he move off. The canine refuses: 'For I noticed – and new life ran through me, life such as terror gives – I noticed from almost invisible indications, which perhaps nobody but myself could have noticed, that in the depths of his chest the hound was preparing to upraise a song. "You're going to sing," I said. "Yes," he said gravely, "I am going to sing, soon, but not yet." "You're beginning it already," I said . . . "I can hear it already, though you deny it," I said trembling . . . the melody, which the hound soon seemed to acknowledge as his, was irresistible . . . But the worst was that it seemed to exist solely for my sake . . .' – once again like the door in 'Before the Law', through which only one man could enter and was closed to him, but which here is open.

This story (with its prohibitions against fasting, which the canine defies, its imposition of silence, which is also defied), though it too is unfinished and full of essential contradictions, is suspended on a positive note.

We might recall that in speaking, in a diary entry of 1911, of what the necessity of writing had emptied him of, what Kafka saw as standing above all else, even sex and eating, was music. Now, what the canine turns to at last as being, for canines, the link between nurture and earth, is 'incantation'; and though music, like fasting, is forbidden, and he has no talent for it, he recognises in his need to pursue the science of music an 'instinct – singular perhaps – but by no means a bad one'.

The dog has previously admitted that 'the only strange thing about me is my nature, yet even that, as I am always careful to remember, has its foundation in universal dog nature'. He is one of those who, like his creator, is 'crushed by the silence, and longs to break through it; literally, to get a breath of fresh air'.

In the final words of this almost final story, Kafka goes beyond anything, I think, in the rest of his writings: 'It was this instinct,' he writes, 'that made me – and perhaps for the sake of science itself, but a different science from that of today, an ultimate science – prize freedom higher than everything else. Freedom! Certainly such freedom as is possible today is a wretched business. But nevertheless freedom, nevertheless a possession.'

Nation Review, *1978*
(revised and expanded, 2010)

THE MIDDLE PARTS OF
FORTUNE – HER PRIVATES WE

*'It is good that a man should throw dice with God
once in his life'*
> *– Frederic Manning, Letter to William
> Rothenstein, July 1916*

FREDERIC MANNING WAS AN Australian from a well-
to-do Catholic family; his father was Lord Mayor of
Sydney. He came to England, aged fifteen, in 1897,
with his tutor Arthur Howard Galton, and lived until
1921 at Edenham near Bourne in Lincolnshire, where
Galton was vicar. A classical scholar, intellectually
refined and disablingly fastidious, he wrote for the
Spectator and Eliot's *Criterion*, was close for a time
to Pound and later to T. E. Lawrence, and between
1907 and 1926 published one long poem, *The Vigil
of Brunhild*, two slim volumes of verse, a series of
imaginary conversations, *Scenes and Portraits*, on
philosophical themes (the conflict between Fate and

individual will), and the introduction to a study of Epicurus. In all ways unlikely, one might have thought, to be the anonymous author of a book whose 'language', when it was published in 1929 – the same year as *All Quiet on the Western Front*, *A Farewell to Arms* and *Goodbye to All That* – caused a minor sensation, and which Hemingway would call 'the finest and noblest book of men in war that I have read'. But then, everything about *The Middle Parts of Fortune* is unlikely.

Between August and December 1916, Manning, already in his middle thirties, had served as a private on the Somme. He wrote *The Middle Parts of Fortune*, in just a few weeks of intense productivity, on the urging of the publisher Peter Davies, to whom it is dedicated: 'To Peter Davies who made me write it'. Davies, who knew his man, took the manuscript 'sheet by sheet' before Manning could re-write it out of existence. 'What an escape!' the author admits. Originally published in a limited edition by 'Private 19022', it was quickly cleaned up for general release under the new title *Her Privates We* and sold fifteen thousand copies in three months. The original text was not reprinted until 1977.

Manning's protagonist, Bourne (we never learn his first name), though educated and a 'gentleman', is a private as Manning was, with no desire for the commission he is so frequently urged to seek. He has friends in England who shower him with parcels, but except for a farmer's wife who sends him a pork pie they are not identified and we hear nothing of Bourne's relations with them. He comes to us, good-humoured and gregarious as he is, with no past history and no evolving history in the present. Manning calls his spirit 'ironic', refers to a 'malicious imp in his heart', and remarks, in passing, that his tendency to take no part in his fellow privates' lively debates springs from a sense of 'isolation . . . since he was not of their county, or their country, or their religion, and he was only partly of their race'. This is both very precise and not, and we hear no more of it. Otherwise we see of Bourne only what belongs to action, observation, reflection in the here and now, with no backward glances.

This is unusual in the central character of a novel; but only perhaps if what we have in mind is the English-language novel of class and character. Manning seems closer here to some of his European contemporaries – Kafka, Musil, Hermann Broch – than to Forster or D. H. Lawrence. For all that *The Middle Parts of Fortune* is so often praised for its realism, its refusal to idealise or conventionalise brute fact, what is more characteristic of Manning is the ease with which he moves from the actual to the abstract or metaphysical; as when, observing the perplexity of men on an exercise that takes them over one landscape as practice for an attack on another, he tells us: 'What they really needed was a map of the strange country through which their minds would travel on the day, with fear darkening earth and filling it with slaughter.'

Among the ranks and classes of the world he finds himself in, Bourne is a free-ranging consciousness – he is welcome everywhere, belongs nowhere, has no preconceptions or previous commitments. The NCOs are happy to use him as a go-between to the officers above and the men below them, and since he is fluent in French to the villages behind the lines, where he acts as their master of revels in organising 'bon times'. With the officers he is sufficiently sensitive to the nuances of caste to feel embarrassed, as they do, when he has to deal with one of them in the presence of an NCO. By nature egalitarian (or is this an aspect of his phantom Australianness?), he never condescends to his fellow privates, and nothing in them disconcerts him: neither their 'Westshire' dialect and obscenities, their opinions, or their exuberant nakedness when one man's throwing off of his uniform in pursuit of an itch sets off a general stripping and a frenetic hunt after lice. His 'bed-chums' are Shem, a Jew (though nothing is made of this: it is a fact that is of no interest to Bourne, or to Manning either) and a larky sixteen-year-old, Martlow, who is somewhat dependent on him.

His sympathy for these men springs from their

shared predicament: 'the desolation and hopelessness of the lunatic world' they are in, the subterranean limbo they move through 'as so many unhouseled ghosts'. It is the absoluteness of this, and the piercing emotion behind it, that makes him, as Hemingway saw, the finest witness we have to that world.

His fellow privates think of themselves as a 'fucken fine mob'. As they prepare quietly for an attack, Bourne makes his own assessment:

The men . . . came from farms, and, in a lesser measure, from mining villages of no great importance. The simplicity of their outlook on life gave them a certain dignity, because it was free from irrelevances. Certainly they had all the appetites of men, and, in the aggregate, probably embodied most of the vices to which flesh is prone; but they were not preoccupied with their vices and appetites, they could master them with rather a splendid indifference; and even sensuality has its aspect of tenderness. These apparently rude and brutal natures comforted, encouraged, and reconciled each other to fate, with a tenderness and tact which was more moving than anything in life . . . They had been brought to the last extremity of hope, and yet they put their hands on each other's shoulders and said with a passionate conviction that it would be all right, though they had faith in nothing, but in themselves and in each other.

What Bourne finds here is the same essentially *sane* view that he has learned to admire in the local peasants: that there is nothing in war which is not in human nature; that the violence and passion it embodies is 'an impersonal and incalculable force . . . which one cannot control, which one cannot understand, and which one can only endure'.

The scenes in which Manning takes us behind the lines, into a world of ordinary domestic life in the presence of women, are among the most appealing and richly comic in the book. When Corporal Greenstreet decides to show off his French and an otherwise obliging housekeeper mistakes his 'cushy' for 'coucher', Bourne has to save his superior from a good box on the ears. Later he is called up in front of the whole brigade to deal with an infuriated woman, 'a very stubborn piece of reality', who storms out 'with her red petticoat kilted up to her knees, her grey stockings, and her ploughman's boots', to defend her clover-patch against a battalion on exercise across her yard.

The appearance of these lone women, including one girl whom Bourne rejects and another to whom he is tenderly drawn, in an all-male world of drinking, swearing, grouching, and 'a state of privation in which men swing between the extremes of sickly sentimentality and a rank obscenity', keeps before us a suspended but unforgotten normality that they all cling to, and a body, all live nerves, that is both innocent and subject to ever-present if inconvenient needs.

*

When *The Middle Parts of Fortune* first appeared it was read as a war novel like any other, an attempt, a decade on, to confront a catastrophe in which citizens in great numbers, some in uniform, many not, had been caught up in a war that was organised in a modern way; that is, on industrial lines. The consensus was that it must never happen again. Close to a century later we have a different perspective.

The Great War was not the 'war to end all wars' but the first in a century of horrors in which untold millions, men, women and children – in battle, in air-raids, in mass executions and eugenic programs, in work-camps, extermination camps and organised famines – would be sacrificed to a murderous abstraction, one or another version of 'History'. This was beyond the comprehension of most First World War writers.

When Sassoon and Owen denounced the war, it was as a sociopolitical phenomenon, a criminal folly. Anger and pity are what Owen is driven to. Manning lacks neither – Bourne's rage over the death of Martlow is Homeric – but war for him is existential; it is simply 'the ultimate problem of all human life stated barely', as he had already faced it, two decades earlier, in the imaginary conversations of *Scenes and Portraits*. How to live nobly if possible, with dignity if possible, in the shadow of imminent extinction. That *The Middle Parts of Fortune* formulates the case in this way, and so clearly, should alert us to something. That as Manning sees it, this is essentially a book about the human predicament.

Still, its context is war and it distinguishes itself as a masterpiece of the genre by leaving nothing unconsidered.

Bourne sees everything he looks at from all sides. The Army is a machine. Within its own terms it is right: it makes plans, promulgates orders, demands discipline. But the men it commands, though they are under arms and accept the fact, are at heart civilians. They see themselves as victims: of injustice, humiliation, institutional blindness, misuse. They too are right. Each man, Bourne observes, sees his own personality as 'something very hard, and sharply defined against a background of other men', who remain 'merely generalised as "the others"'. This too is right; it is one of the strategies for survival, and Bourne recognises it as his own. But Manning is a writer. It is his business to bring these others in out of the realm of the generalised and make them as actual to Bourne, and to us, as they are to themselves.

Each of the battalion officers in the book – Mr

Clinton, Mr Malet, Mr Marsden, Mr Finch – has his unique temperament and style, and the same is true of the NCOs – Corporal (later Sergeant) Tozer, Lance Corporal Johnson, Corporals Greenstreet and Hamley – and the men: Shem, Martlow, 'Weeper' Smart.

Bourne too is seen from all sides; judged in the light of each man's specialist concern. 'When 'e first came to us,' Sergeant Tozer tells Mr Malet, 'we took 'im for a dud, but after a few days 'e seemed quite able to take care of 'imself; fact I thought 'e might be gettin' a bit fresh an' decided to keep an eye on 'im. I couldn't find any fault with 'im.' Mr Malet thinks he has too much influence over the men, 'and has no business to'. 'Weeper' Smart, seeing Mr Marsden intimidate Bourne into volunteering for a raid, and recalling an occasion when Bourne insisted he take a fair share of the champagne he was doling out, though he himself had 'nowt to share', tells him angrily: 'When 'a seed that fucken' slave-driver look at 'ee, 'a said, A'm comin'. A'll always say this for thee, th'll share all th'ast got wi' us'uns, and don't call a man by any foolish nick-names.'

Again and again here, 'men are bound together more closely by the trivial experiences they have shared than by the most sacred obligations'. This takes Manning immediately to the heart of things.

A man called Pritchard's bed-chum is killed.

''E were dyin' so quick you could see it . . . "'Elp me up," he sez, "'elp me up." "You lie still, chum," I sez to 'im, "you'll be right presently." "An he jes gives me one look, like 'e were puzzled, an 'e died.'

'Well anyway,' said Martlow, desperately comforting, ''e couldn't 'ave felt much, could 'e, if 'e said that?'

'I don't know what 'e felt,' said Pritchard, with slowly filling bitterness, 'I know what I felt.'

Manning has been to school with Tolstoy and Shakespeare, who provides, in a collaboration that does honour to both, an epigraph for each chapter of Manning's book. No man here is denied his moment on the page.

When Bourne hears that a man called Bates has been killed 'he tried to remember who Bates was; and at the effort of memory to recover him, he seemed to hear a high excited voice suddenly cry out, as though actually audible to the whole dugout. "What's 'e want to drag me into 't for!" And it was as though Bates were bodily present there . . . He knew no more of Bill Bates than that phrase, passionately innocent: "What's 'e want to drag me into 't for!"'

In a late moment with Martlow, Bourne realises that if he were to become an officer he would have 'to forget a lot; and even as he was thinking how impossible it would be to forget, Martlow looked up at him with a grin on his puckish face . . . and already his memory was haunted by outstretched hands seeking rescue from oblivion, and faces half-submerged to which he could give no name.' Then, on the next word, Manning supplies the name: '*Martlow* only grinned more broadly'.

Earlier, dropping off to sleep between Martlow and Shem, Bourne had wondered 'what was the spiritual thing in them which lived, and seemed to grow stronger, in beastliness?'

It is this spiritual thing that Manning is after, and which shines out in even the darkest pages of his book. To bear witness to the brutality and tenderness of war is only part of it. 'There is,' he tells us, 'an extraordinary veracity in war that strips man of every conventional covering he has, and leaves him to face a fact as naked and inexorable as himself.'

It is that naked, inexorable fact, and the power with which Manning in page after page makes it real, that sets *The Middle Parts of Fortune* beside the best of Mann, Kafka, Hamsun, Camus, Beckett, among the indisputable classics of its century.

Introduction to The Middle Parts of Fortune, *Folio Society, 2012*

THE QUICK OF THINGS:
LAWRENCE AND WALT WHITMAN

A GOOD MANY WRITERS of fiction have also in the course of a busy writing life produced memorable poems, George Meredith for one, Thackeray for another, and several poets have produced single novels that stand as undisputed masterpieces: one thinks immediately of Goldsmith's *The Vicar of Wakefield*, Lermontov's *A Hero of Our Time*, Mörike's novella, *Mozart's Journey to Prague*. But few writers have an equal reputation in both fields: Goethe in Germany, Pushkin in Russia, Hugo in France; in England Hardy, maybe Kipling.

D. H. Lawrence is surely one of the few. In a frenetic publishing life, and during many moves – from England to Germany in 1912, and on to Italy; to Australia, Mexico and the United States in the 1920s, and finally to Spain and the south of France – he worked simultaneously, and always at the highest intensity, on novels, poems, travel books, criticism, reviews. There is no time after he began in 1909 when his notebooks are not filled with poems, and no time in his publishing life when he is not, between novels and volumes of short stories, either preparing collections of poems or seeing them through the press.

This needs careful tracking. Postage, because of his travels, forms part of the story, and so does accident. So does interference or confiscation by the customs authorities in the cause of public decency. There are multiple typescripts and the fact that Lawrence was seldom at hand when the poems were being edited means that many of the publications are corrupt. They may also differ for another reason.

Because of Lawrence's subjects, and the language he uses, many of the poems were at the last moment expurgated by the publisher or withdrawn, not always after consultation with Lawrence himself (again the matter of distance) and not always with his consent.

All this is thoroughly dealt with in the new Cambridge Edition in two volumes, edited by Christopher Pollnitz: one for the poems and Lawrence's prefaces to the various collections (this is the first complete and corrected edition of the poems), a second for the vast critical apparatus such an undertaking involves: the variant versions, notes on each poem and on the publication of each book and its reception – even a note on pounds, shillings and pence.

*

Each lover of Lawrence's poems will have his own story of first contact with a new and unique consciousness.

Lawrence was the first entirely modern poet I was presented with, and except for what I had picked up from films – the accidental influence, in Hollywood movies of the late thirties and early forties, of German Expressionist theatre and décor and, on the soundtrack, German contemporary music – the first modernist sensibility. I was twelve, going on thirteen, in my first months at Brisbane Grammar.

As the bright Latin form, we were already skilled at the sort of analysis and parsing that was the regular drill in Queensland primary schools, so we did nothing in our English class but read. The Lawrence poem in our class anthology was 'Snake', and it was like no other poem I had ever heard – I say heard because poetry always began in those days as a reading aloud. I did with it immediately what I had been encouraged to do with any poem that in some way struck me, or which puzzled or eluded me. I got its music into my head (*prima la musica*), and its logic, or lack of logic, by learning it off by heart. Like many poems learned by heart at that time, it is still with me.

What mesmerised me was the poem's rhythms, and the perfect ease with which the lines, long or short, contained each thought and added it to the 'story'. And the openness of that story as confession, Lawrence's readiness, with no hint of self-consciousness or posing, to give himself away. I had never come across anything like that either. I took it as a kind of lesson in how I might deal with my own feelings, even the ones I was ashamed of.

In learning the poem by heart, what it had to tell – the experience it embodied but also the rhythm of its discoveries, each one as it arrived – became mine; I had made it mine, along with the voice that expressed it. This might have robbed the thing, through easy familiarity, of its challenges. Instead, odd lines, in my head as they now were, stood out suddenly and confronted me so that I had to confront them.

'The voices of my education said to me / He must be killed.' But Lawrence did not want to kill the creature. Could the voices of our education be wrong? – I had never been presented with *that* idea. And clearly, in this case, they *were* wrong. In attacking the snake Lawrence had sinned. But wasn't the serpent the very embodiment of sin? *This* serpent, in opposition to what the Bible asserted, was holy, because it was another creature like us, part of a Creation that was also holy – was that it? So the Bible was mistaken on that score also. Everything in the poem seemed to question and reverse what I had till now been told. There was a new sort of pleasure in this. Each line as it turned was full of surprise and discovery.

There is a good deal in that schoolboy response that I would stand by still, and re-reading the poems in *Birds, Beasts and Flowers* (1923), I experienced again, in their simple-seeming but complex statements, line after line, the same discomfort and release of that twelve-year-old. But what strikes me now is how carefully prepared I had been to meet this challenge by all those long afternoons with our State School Readers; through the three weeks we had spent on the *Rime of the Ancient Mariner* in Grade Seven, and our explorations, in Grade Six, in the story of Pluto and Persephone (along with Lord Leighton's vivid illustration), of the pagan underworld that Lawrence was evoking, and inviting me, if I was daring enough, to recognise as my world also and share:

And I thought of the albatross
And I wished he would come back, my snake.
For he had seemed to me again like a king,
Like a king in exile, uncrowned in the underworld,
Now due to be crowned again.
And so I had missed my chance with one of the lords
of Life.

*

Lawrence's move – between September 1920, when he writes the first poems in *Birds, Beasts and Flowers*, and the completion of the manuscript in February 1923 – from a strictly human and personal world into the world of the creatures, is an extraordinary liberation.

These winged, beaked, taloned creatures, these slow-moving earth-creatures with carapace shells, and fish, bats, snakes, mosquitos – nature's fantastic work of invention and play; these infinite variations on a life force that responds, with every condition of large and small, of quick and slow, in designs of so much surprise and utility and grace, call up in Lawrence a similar spirit of playful and inventive *making*. In his own version of creative fantasy, and with the liveliest humour and wit, he becomes a psalmist and celebrant of the animist creed – lyric, parodic, lightly critical; a master of reflexive attention; an imitator of nature's own utilitarian caprice.

No more brooding on whether or not he is loved. No more stewing over the smallness of human needs and views, or the way 'mind' perverts and desecrates the purities of sensation. The creatures are above or beyond all that. Their world is all instinct and immediacy, but clean, and since they know nothing of the moralities, it is also guiltless. The joy Lawrence takes in their otherness is childlike, as Blake's was; of a kind where innocence is a state beyond experience, but where one needs to come *through* experience to reach it. He never puts a foot wrong. Rhythm and cadence both follow and preclude sense, and contain and fix it. Entering *into* becomes a form of reflection, but also of self-reflection, each encounter producing its own tone and truth:

> When did you start your tricks,
> Monsieur?
> . . . Are you one too many for me
> Winged Victory?
> Am I not mosquito enough to out-mosquito you?
>
> 'Mosquito'

> Your life a sluice of sensation along your sides
> . . . joie de vivre, and fear, and food,
> All without love.
> To have the element under you like a lover
> I didn't know his God.
> I didn't know his God.
> Which is perhaps the last admission that life has to
> wring out of us.
>
> 'Fish'

> A twitch, a twitter, an elastic shudder in flight.
> In China the bat is symbol of happiness.
> Not for me!
>
> 'Bat'

Challenger,
Little Ulysses, fore-runner,
No bigger than my thumb-nail,
Buon viaggio.
All animate creation on your shoulder,
Set forth, little Titan, under your battle-shield.

'Baby Tortoise'

Alas, the spear is through the side of his isolation.
His adolescence saw him crucified into sex,
Damned, in the long crucifixion of desire, to seek
His consummation beyond himself . . .
Doomed to make an intolerable fool of himself
In his effort toward completion again.
And so behold him following the tail
Of that mud-hovel of his slowly rambling spouse.

'Elle et Lui'

Still, gallant, irascible, crooked-legged reptile,
Little gentleman,
Sorry plight,
We ought to look the other way.

'Tortoise Gallantry'

*

Lawrence's work on *Birds, Beasts and Flowers*, from the first free-verse notes of July 1920, through the

Tortoise poems of September and 'Snake' in 1921, to the 'new, "complete" MS' of February 1923, coincided with his various attempts to produce the essay on Walt Whitman that was to form the final chapter of his *Studies in Classic American Literature* (1923). It was because Whitman was so important to him that the essay gave him so much trouble, and it is in Lawrence's attempts to get at the 'quick' of Whitman's practice – what he sees as the origin and process, physical and psycho-sexual, of it – that we see what Lawrence was aiming at in his own: the process, but also, in moral and aesthetic terms (which increasingly for Lawrence became one), its justification.

The first version from 1918 has not survived, and so far as we know, no-one ever saw it. It was too controversial, perhaps, in its openness about the sensual life. The 1919 version immediately adopts a combative stance:

Whitman is the last and greatest of the Americans. He is the fulfilment of the great old truth. But any truth, the moment it is fulfilled, accomplished, becomes *ipso facto* a lie, a deadly limitation of truth . . . In Whitman lies the greatest of all modern truths. And yet some really thoughtful men, in Europe at least, insist even today that he is the greatest of modern humbugs, the arch humbug. A great truth – or a great lie – which? A great prophet, or a great swindle.

Both!

Lawrence has no doubts about the quality and significance of Whitman's verse. 'The primal soul,' he tells us,

> utters itself in strange pulsations, gushes and strokes of sound. At his best Whitman gives these throbs naked and vibrating as they emerge from the quick. They follow, pulse after pulse, line after line, each one new and unforeseeable. They are lambent. They are life itself. But in the whole, the whole soul speaks at once, sensual impulse instant with spiritual impulse, and the mind serving, giving pure attention.

This is also, we may assume, how Lawrence hopes his own verse, at its best, may work. It is a matter of the relationship between the lower or sensual body and the mind, with the mind serving, and in it here that he sees Whitman, in that he chooses finally the way of 'sensual negation', failing to take 'the next step'. The language in which he describes Whitman's failure to complete the process is drawn from *Fantasia of the Unconscious*, a book already completed but not to be published until October 1922.

> Whitman, singing of the mystery of touch, tells us of the process. He tells of the mystery of the touch of the hands and fingers, those living tendrils of the upper spiritual centres, upon the lower body. But the

touch of the hands is only the beginning of a great involved process. Not only the fingers reap the deep forces, but the mouth and tongue in kissing and so on . . . All this Whitman minutely and continually describes. It is the transferring to the upper centres, the thorasic and cervical ganglia, of the control of the deep lumbar and sacral ganglia, it is the transferring to the upper sympathetic centres, breast, hands, mouth, face, of the dark vital secrets of the lower self. The lower sacral centres are explored and *known* by the upper self.

It is this transferring of everything into the realm of *knowing*, into the upper self and the 'mental consciousness', that makes Whitman, for Lawrence, 'a shattering half-truth, a devastating half-lie'.

He also falls short in another respect. 'Every soul,' Lawrence insists, 'before it can be free, and whole in itself, spontaneously blossom[ing] from itself, must know this accession into Allness, into infinitude. Thus far Whitman is a great prophet. And he shows us the process of oneing; he is a true prophet.' The falseness creeps in when we accept this 'oneing' as a goal in itself, and not as the means to a different end, which in Lawrence's terms – as he had been working towards it in *Look! We Have Come Through!* (1917), in 'New Heaven and Earth' and 'Manifest' and 'Wedlock', for example – is 'the human soul's integral singleness':

And yet all the while you are you, you are not me.
And I am I, I am never you.
How awfully distinct and far off from each other's
being we are.
Yet I am glad.
I am glad there is always you beyond my scope.

What Lawrence rejects in Whitman is the insistence on 'merging', on 'fusion'. Lawrence himself aims at something different. He calls it a 'delicately adjusted polarity'.

There is a final polarisation, a final current of vital being impossible(e) between man and woman. Whitman found this empirically. Empirically he found that the last current of vital polarisation goes between man and man. Whitman is the first in modern life, truly, from sheer empirical necessity, to reassert this truth . . . It is his most wistful theme – the love of comrades – manly love . . . The vast mysterious power of sexual love and of marriage is not for Whitman . . . He believes in fusion. Not fusion, but delicately adjusted polarity is life. Fusion is death.

Still, there is, beyond all this, Whitman's verse. There, at its best, 'the whole soul follows its own free, spontaneous, inexplicable course, the contractions and pulsations dictated from nowhere save from the quick itself . . . There is nothing measured or mechanical. This is the greatest poetry.'

But even this statement of the case is not satisfactory and in 1921–22 Lawrence sets out to resolve his own contradictory views in yet another version. 'Whitman,' he begins, 'is the last and greatest of the Americans. One of the greatest poets in the world, in him an element of falsity troubles us still. Something is wrong; we cannot be quite at ease with his greatness. Let us get over our quarrel with him first.' He then goes on to make a distinction between

> all the transcendentalists, including Whitman, and men like Balzac and Dickens, Tolstoy and Hardy, who still act direct from passional motives and not inversely, from mental provocations. But the aesthetes and symbolists, from Baudelaire and Maeterlinck, and Oscar Wilde onwards, and nearly all the later Russian and French and English novelists, set up their reactions in the mind and reflect them by a secondary process down on the body. It is the madness of the world today. Europe and America are all alike, all the nations self-consciously provoking their passional reactions from the mind, and *nothing* spontaneous.

The last part of this version then moves into the murky area of mystical fascism. Whitman, Lawrence tells us, shows us the last step of the old great way. But he does not show us the first step of the new. His great Democracy is to be established upon the love of comrades. Well and good. But in what direction shall this love flow? More *en masse*? As a matter of fact the love of comrades is always a love between a leader and a follower filled with 'the joy of liege adherence'.

What Lawrence ends up saluting, in a move away from 'en masse democracy' to 'the grand culmination of soul-chosen leaders', is 'the final leader . . . the sacred *tyrannus*. This is the true democracy.' 'Onward,' he urges, 'always following the leader, who when he looks back has a flame of love in his face, but a still brighter flame of purpose. This is the true democracy.'

Whitman, at this point, is largely forgotten. The best Lawrence can do is to repeat his earlier endorsement:

Whitman. The last of the very great poets. And the ultimate. How lovely a poet he is. His verse at its best spontaneous like a bird. For a bird doesn't rhyme or scan – the miracle of spontaneity. The whole soul speaks at once, in a naked spontaneity so unutterably lovely, so far beyond rhyme and scansion.

Then, in November 1922, a new version in an entirely different style: demotic, staccato, 'Modernist'; all capitals, expletives and ironic or dismissive side-swipes;

a parody of Whitman's own 'stridency' and splenetic exuberance:

> Post mortem effects?
> But what of Walt Whitman?
> The 'good grey poet'
> Was he a ghost, with all his physicality?
> The good grey poet
> Post mortem effects. Ghosts.
> A certain ghoulishness. A certain horrible potage of human parts. A certain stridency and portentousness. A luridness about his beatitudes . . .
> I AM HE THAT ACHES WITH AMOROUS LOVE
> CHUFF! CHUFF! CHUFF!
> CHU-CHU-CHU-CHU-CHUFFF
> Reminds me of a steam engine. A locomotive . . .
> Your Self
> Oh Walter, Walter, what have you done with it? What have you done with yourself? With your individual self? For it sounds as if it had all leaked out of you when you made water, leaked into the universe when you peed. Oh Walt, you're a leaky vessel . . .

And so on, via a piece of scurrilous gossip about Whitman in old age dancing naked in his yard and showing himself off in an excited state to school-girls, to

Only we know this much. Death is not the *goal*. And Love, and merging are now only part of the death process. Comradeship – part of the death process. The new Democracy – the brink of death. One identity – death itself.

We have died, and we are still disintegrating.

But IT is finished.

Consumatum est.

At which point the essay degenerates into incoherent rambling about Jesus and the Holy Ghost. Barely a word in this version about Whitman the poet. Only Whitman, the leaky vessel, as thinker and man.

The 1923 version, the one that at last makes it all the way to publication as the final chapter of *Studies in Classic American Literature*, takes up the 1922 version and uses it – expurgated of its scurrilous slander and a few turns of phrase that would at the time have been seen as 'indecent' – as far as 'But IT is finished. *Consumatum est.*' It then drops its expletive tone and embarks on something more sober and considered, more warmly personal:

Whitman, the great poet, has meant much to me. Whitman the one man breaking a way ahead. Whitman the one pioneer. And only Whitman. No English pioneers, no French. In Europe the would-be pioneers are mere improvisers.

He recognises Whitman as 'the first to smash the old moral conception that the soul of man is something "superior" and "above" the flesh'.

'There,' he said to the soul, 'stay there! Stay there. Stay in the flesh. Stay in the limbs and legs and in the belly. Stay in the breast and womb and phallus. Stay there, o soul, where you belong.'

There is praise too for Whitman's enunciation of 'a morality of actual living, not of salvation':

The soul is not to put up defences round herself. She is not to withdraw inwardly, in mystical ecstasies, she is not to cry to some God beyond, for salvation. She is to go down the open road, as the road opens into the unknown, keeping company with those whose soul draws them near to her, accomplishing nothing save the journey . . . The Open Road. The great home of the soul is the open road. Not heaven, not paradise. Not 'above', not even 'within'. The soul is neither 'above' nor 'within'. It is a wayfarer down the open road . . . The soul is herself when she is going on foot down the open road.

He even forgives Whitman at this point his great error, of mistaking 'sympathy' for Jesus' Love or St Paul's Charity. But he has arrived now at a more doctrinaire vision of what art itself is, what poetry is, that from this point will determine his own life as a poet:

> The function of art is moral. Not aesthetic, not decorative, not pastime and recreation. But moral . . . But a passionate, implicit morality, not didactic. Changes the blood rather than the mind, changes the blood first. The mind follows later, in the wake.

This looks ahead to the various prefaces Lawrence would write, between Christmas 1928 and April 1929, to *Pansies* (1929) – Pensées – the second of which tells us:

> Each little piece is a thought: not an idea, or an opinion, or a didactic statement, but a true thought, which comes as much from the heart and genitals as from the head . . . Live and let live, and each pansy will tip you its separate wink.

*

Between 1923 and November 17, 1928, when *Pansies* was begun, Lawrence was continually on the move, in Mexico, England, France, Italy; at work preparing ('what a sweat'), and in the case of the earlier poems, rewriting, his *Collected Poems* (1928). 'I do bits of things,' he writes on November 14, 1927, '– darn my underclothes, try to type up poems.'

The *Pansies*, written at Bandol on the French Riviera between November 17, 1928, and March 10, 1929, and the 'stinging pansies' or *Nettles* (1930), which he began in February 1929 and took up again between April 17 and June 18 in Mallorca, start out as insights into the quick of things – sensory moments, the lives of elephants in a circus – but end up in disgruntlement and general contempt for 'the dirty drab world': its hypocrisy, cowardice, snobbery, money-grubbing; its blindness and vanity – 'the whole damn swindle'. Then, on October 10, 1929, just five months before his death, he writes the first poem in the *Last Poems* (1932) notebook, 'The Greeks Are Coming', and we might recall what he had written of Whitman: 'Whitman would not have been the great poet he is if he had not taken the last step and looked over into Death.'

There are hints, towards the end of the *Nettles* notebook, of Lawrence's last poems: in 'Butterfly' (I) and (II), in 'The State of Grace', and 'Glory of Darkness' (I), which is in fact an early version of 'Bavarian Gentians':

Blue and dark
the Bavarian Gentians, tall ones
make a magnificent dark-blue gloom

in the sunny room . . .
How deep I have gone
dark gentians
in your marvellous dark-blue godhead
How deep, how deep, how happy
How happy to sink my soul
in the blue dark gloom
of gentian here in the sunny room!

'Glory of Darkness' (I)

But it is 'Glory of Darkness' (III) that takes the final step and finds its way back to the Greeks, to the old dark underworld of 'Snake':

Blue and dark
Oh Bavarian gentians, tall ones . . .
They have added blueness to blueness, until
it is dark beauty, it is dark
and the door is open
to the depths
It is so blue, it is so dark
in the dark doorway
and the door is open
to Hades.
Oh I know –
Persephone has just gone back
down the thickening thickening gloom
of dark blue gentians

to Pluto
to her bridegroom
in the dark . . .

'Glory of Darkness' (III)

And with the simplicity, the spontaneity of this – what he called, in Whitman's case, its 'throbs and pulses' – Lawrence finds his way to the poems on which his own greatness rests.

God is older than the sun and moon
and the eye cannot behold him
nor voice describe him.
But a naked man, a stranger, leaned on the gate
with his cloak over his arm waiting to be asked in.
So I called him: Come in, if you will –
He came in slowly, and sat down by the hearth.
I said to him: And what is your name? –
He looked at me without answer, but such a loveliness
entered me, I smiled to myself, saying: he is God!
So he said: *Hermes*!
God is older than the sun and moon
and the eye cannot behold him
nor the voice describe him:
and still, this is the god Hermes, sitting by my
    hearth.

'Maximus'

Lawrence is a difficult poet to come to terms with; it is easy to quarrel with him as he quarrelled with Whitman. He is various, contradictory, irascible, over-insistent; he too easily takes offence and insists again. It is easy, as well, to be put off by his preachiness. He begins in the tone of a nonconformist Bible-banger, then develops his own religion and bangs away at that. He is most easy with his soul when he embraces the dark gods and goes quietly underground, and best of all when he stops protesting and lets the world in, in the form of a snake, a baby tortoise, the smoking dark blue of gentians, or in the form of the psychopomp Hermes, and breathes easy again. Lets the breath, and the energy of its natural rhythms, create the poem.

As he puts it in the Note to *Collected Poems* of May 12, 1928, excusing his rewriting of the early poems, 'A young man is afraid of his demon, and puts his hand over his demon's mouth and speaks for him. And the things the young man says are rarely poetry. So I have tried to let the demon say his say.'

Lawrence makes it difficult for the reader, as well as for himself, by speaking up too soon; by performing; working out his questions, his quarrels, in public. We too, in seeking out the best in him, have to choose between the 'demon' and the man.

At his best, Lawrence, like Whitman, is one of the finest poets in the world. There is no poet, at his best, who gets closer to what he calls the 'quick' of things, or brings us closer with him; and when he is at ease with his own spirit, his own extraordinary energy, his rare demon, there is no poet we find it so easy to love. It is all here in these two hefty volumes: the muddle, but also the magic of the man's greatness; the pathos, the wonderful coincidence of language and feeling; a sensibility almost too actively aware of the tension between singularity and oneness that is at the heart of being.

Sydney Review of Books, *2013*

PERILOUS TENSION:
THE YOUNG DESIRE IT

THE YOUNG DESIRE IT was published in London in
1937 by Jonathan Cape. The author, Kenneth 'Seaforth'
Mackenzie, was not quite twenty-four. He had begun
the novel at seventeen. 'Five weeks of solitude,' he tells
us in a dedicatory preface, 'saw the making of the whole
thing.'

Like many first novels, *The Young Desire It* draws
on the author's own experience. Mackenzie grew up
on an isolated property north of Perth, and until he
entered Guildford Grammar at thirteen shared the
company only of his mother, a younger sister and a few
household servants. He was left to roam, barefoot and
as he pleased, in the local countryside, whose changes
of light and weather he seems to have taken, like his
protagonist Charles Fox, as aspects of his own nature
and feelings. This accounts the intensity of the
book's nature writing, which is more disciplined than

anything in Lawrence, who is clearly an influence, but also more inward and passionately lyrical. Charles Fox's first encounter with society, in the close, intrusive and sometimes threatening form of a boys' boarding school, accounts for his puzzled outsider's view of his fellow students and teachers. What is not accounted for in so young a writer is the authority with which he tackles the book's disturbing and potentially sensational material, and the assurance, in the rhythm and cadence of every sentence, of the writing. We recognise the phenomenon, but it is rare, in the precocious genius of Stephen Crane in *The Red Badge of Courage*, in the young Thomas Mann of *Buddenbrooks*, and the even younger Raymond Radiguet of *Le Diable au Corps* and *Le Bal du Comte d'Orgel*. Mackenzie and *The Young Desire It* are of their company.

The novel has two points of focus.

One is the school as a social institution: in this case an English-style, all-male boarding school in what is still, in the twenties, an outpost of empire; an establishment devoted to the making, through classical studies, music, sport, and very British notions of manliness and public service, of young men.

The masters are imported Englishmen, the students for the most part country boys who have grown up close to the Australian bush and to Australian values and traditions. They are lively and well meaning enough, but from the masters' point of view uncultivated, even when, like Charles Fox, they are also sensitive and talented. In the course of the book the whole order and ethos of the school is tested by the suicide of a wounded, yet highly effective and revered headmaster.

It is worth recalling that at this time most boys of fourteen or fifteen were already out in the world earning a living. A good part of Charles Fox's impatience to be done with school, and free, is a belief that he is being held back from life, though he also acknowledges that he knows little of what life is. He has till now been a kind of 'wild child' armed only with 'a dangerous innocence' and unaware of 'the necessity for doing evil'. How he comes through – whether in fact he does come through – is the book's other and major concern.

On his first afternoon at the school he is sexually assaulted by a group of older boys, on the pretext of confirming that this pretty boy is not really a girl. What Charles discovers here, as a first line of defence, is a quality in himself, to this point unknown because unneeded, that will more and more become the keynote of his emerging character. This is resistance, which over time takes different forms in him, not all of them attractive. Resistance to others, and to events and influence; resistance to his own need for affection; a growing hardness that will protect him from being 'interfered with', and allow him the freedom – it is freedom of choice that the young so ardently desire – to be himself.

Several moments of revelation mark the course of Charles' adolescent progress, some of them so deeply interiorised and undramatic as to appear, by conventional novelistic standards, unrealised: a common complaint against *The Young Desire It* is that it is a book in which, as Douglas Stewart puts it, 'nothing happens'.

Another way of putting it would be to suggest that Mackenzie, in a quite revolutionary way for an Australian writer in the late thirties, is doing all he can to preserve his narrative from any whiff of the 'fictitious', and himself from any temptation to the fabrications of 'plot'. What interests him is not what happens in the world of events but what happens in Charles Fox's erotically charged sensory world, where he is confronted at every turn with situations for which he has no precedent. It is Mackenzie's determination to stick with the interior view, and the bewilderments of young Charles Fox, that make *The Young Desire It* perhaps the earliest novel in Australia to deal with the inner life in a consistently modernist way. Patrick White's *The Aunt's Story* is still a decade off.

The most significant of Charles Fox's discoveries is his meeting, on his first vacation, with the schoolgirl Margaret.

Essential to this is that it happens on Charles' home

ground. The mystery of the occasion is bound up with the secret, half-underground quality of the place, with its low-hanging pine branches, damp pine needles, misty rain. The fact that it is grounded in the boy's sensuous inner world means he can take for granted that what is so shatteringly 'final' for him is equally so for the girl, and it is this that makes 'impossible' for Charles the next significant moment of the book, when, back at school, Penworth, the young classics master he has formed a bond with, kisses him.

Charles has suffered a fainting fit in the school gym at the sight of his friend Mawley's twisted ankle. When he comes to he is in Penworth's room, on Penworth's bed, with Penworth sitting on the bed beside him, clasping his feet in his 'broad hands'. Confused by this but not yet anxious, he allows himself to be drawn into a discussion of his dreams, then confesses his ignorance, beyond the crude schoolboy facts, of what such dreams might mean, and of all sexual matters. The kiss that follows turns the boy's confusion to alarm.

He is in no danger, he knows that. This is a proposal, not an assault, and anything beyond this is to him an 'impossibility' – he has already had his revelation with Margaret; it is final and of another kind. What concerns him now is how he should act so that his response, while clearly a rejection, will allow him to retain Penworth's affectionate interest, and Penworth his self-esteem.

The man is gently reassuring: 'It's all right, dear lad . . . Don't be frightened – I shan't hurt you . . . Were you frightened of – something that might have happened?'

But it is the boy who shows the greater care. 'I may not know it all, but even if I am so young,' he tells Penworth, 'I do know that you're unhappy; and if I could help I would.' As Mackenzie has observed earlier, this is a school 'where many of the boys are old for their years and many of the Masters seem young for theirs'.

It is the delicacy with which Mackenzie negotiates the difficulties here that is remarkable: the way we see Penworth; the way Penworth sees himself; the extent to which the narrator stands clear of judgement.

On Charles' first night in the dormitory, Penworth, as duty master, has stepped in on a scene of bathroom bullying and is surprised, when he tumbles Charles out of a laundry basket, by the shock to his senses of the boy's nakedness. What the moment uncovers in him is entirely unexpected.

Later, after the 'hard, clumsy kiss', the scenes between the two are full of tension, but of different kinds, though they spring from the same cause: loneliness among the proximities of communal living, and an uncertainty in the school's culture about the distance that should be kept between masters and boys.

On Charles' side there is his unwillingness to hurt Penworth, but also his own need for contact: 'the goodness of having such a friend, so quickly in sympathy . . . was a warm glow in his heart'. On Penworth's a growing confusion at 'the warm desires, complex, multiplied, and ceaselessly relevant to his awareness of the boy'.

Later again, disappointed and out of control after he has trapped Charles into revealing his secret – the relationship with Margaret – Penworth moves on from formal schoolmasterly banter and accuses Charles, in front of the whole class, of being one of those who set themselves above the rest 'because Nature has by mistake given them pretty faces and pretty ways, and has further erred in making them aware of her unfortunate gifts'.

When Charles, as ordered, comes to see him afterwards and gives way to 'childish hysterics', Penworth finds himself 'enjoying the curious sensation of his secret shame and elation, and above all enjoying now that supreme and most godly power, the power to comfort when his dramatic sense permitted comfort'. Penworth has had his own revelation, a dark one: 'He could not see the anguish he had brought into the boy's face without seeing also that it was as true as his own pretended coldness was false and cruel. Yet the pain he watched gave him a surge of – was that pleasure?'

There is not much Australian fiction, of this or any other time, that ventures into such uneasy territory, and works so powerfully there. Penworth, weak, inexperienced, emotionally undeveloped, out of place in a country so unlike his own, painfully devoted to 'that eternal tenant of the mind, Reason', but increasingly vulnerable to passions that he recognises from his classical studies but has never expected to be touched by, is the book's most complex character and in some ways its most complete achievement. He is awed by, as well as attracted to Charles Fox, whom he recognises, for all his youth, as nobler and more manly than himself. His angry disappointment has less to do with Charles' rejection of his advances than with his realisation that this boy, at barely fifteen, has already come to what he himself yearns for but has still to attain: the perfect communion he had hoped a relationship with the boy might at last bring him.

There is disappointment for Charles as well. He preserves his relationship with Penworth but is increasingly wary of him. More significantly he sees in the man a likeness now to his mother that makes him distrustful of her as well: a quality, in someone whose affection he has come to rely on, that is not pure care but a wish, under the guise of care, to steal from him his life, his youth. For the first time he applies to his mother his newfound resistance, and she in turn warns him, in terms that are chilling in their prescience of Mackenzie's own future, against the man who has abandoned them both. 'Your father,' she tells him, 'always went to extremes. If he was happy, or miserable, I always thought he was too much so. He let himself go completely . . . It made him drink to forget; and drink took him away from me – from us. Took him away from you; that's what I mind most.'

The question that arises is less the degree to which Mackenzie is drawing on his own experience for Charles Fox – that is clear – than how far, in the writing, he moves away from it.

The Young Desire It is a third-person narrative but of a peculiar sort. By settling on a single consciousness and a deeply interior point of view, it becomes in effect a first-person narrative in third-person form. At least, that is how it begins. But fifty pages in a new perspective is introduced, that of Charles' classmate Mawley. We never quite enter into Mawley's consciousness as we do Charles' – his is an observatory rather than a reflective intelligence, but one of the objects of his scrutiny is Charles himself, and while Mawley never becomes either a fully developed character or actor in the book, he may, in the end, be its real narrator.

It is Mawley's accident in the gym that causes Charles to faint, and Mawley's need to remain in the school sick bay over the vacation (while Charles is engaged on his second meeting with Margaret) takes up a good part of the middle section of the book.

Each evening Mawley is visited by the headmaster, and in the shared isolation and loneliness of the empty school a kind of friendship develops between them:

> It was impossible not to be drawn closer under the kindly shadow of his great personality; he did indeed seem young, with the essence of youth, with all its ability to feel, quick and deep, the drama of fortune's ceaseless mutation; without youth's clumsiness of thought or speech to divide Mawley from him. The boy's sympathy was not of embarrassment but of what, thought he in his pride, was genuine understanding.

This is an ideal version of a relationship of which Penworth's approaches to Charles are an unhappy distortion. The confidences offered when the headmaster settles on the edge of Mawley's bed, which are intimate enough, stand in stark contrast to the exchanges between Penworth and Charles that lead up to the kiss.

On the last of his visits, on the eve of his suicide, the headmaster speaks of love and the responsibilities of the lover. 'Once,' he tells Mawley,

> when I was young, someone said to me in reproof for some thoughtlessness, 'You must learn how easy it is to hurt those you love . . .' Then, I believed that;

afterwards I found that it was not true, for it is easiest to hurt those who love you – those you yourself love may not be open to harm from you. But if they in turn love you, then beware.

In the early forties, Mackenzie, writing to Jane Lindsay, offered this version of his time at Guildford Grammar:

When I was at school I, being angel-faced and slim and shy, was apparently considered fair game by masters as well as certain boys. The boys were at least honestly crude in their proposals; but the masters – young men whom I thought very mature and wise – had a much better technique. They wooed the intellectual way, just at the very time I was beginning to comprehend something of literature and music, and so was most gullible. Again and again, like any simpleton, I was tricked, only to realise that what I had taken for special interest in possible intellectual promise of mine was not that at all.

This was written nearly fifteen years after the event and after a good deal of disappointment and disintegration; Mackenzie is in some ways making excuses for himself. But the important point is that the bitterness of this account is nowhere to be found in the novel. He goes on:

My whole psyche was shaped by those years – first living with women only, then living entirely separated from anything womanly, and with my unfortunate appearance and the fact that I had a boy's soprano singing voice and was Chapel soloist (another cause of disgusting molestation) . . . All these long-drawn-out circumstances conditioned me mentally, emotionally and – I don't doubt – sexually.

It is true that Charles Fox at the end of *The Young Desire It* is no longer so innocently open and attractive as he was at the beginning. We may even see in him the makings of a man whose course of life is to be 'difficult'. The last glimpse we get of him is not quite optimistic.

Seen through Mawley's eyes when he returns to school for his second and final year, Charles seems easier with the world, or so Mawley thinks.

What Mawley does not know is that in another of his secret places Charles and Margaret, with 'the air stretched to a perilous tension, ready to split and shatter, ready with the whole world to burst into flame', have consummated their love, not as errant, under-aged children but 'by blind volition of their own single will'. They have also parted and may not meet again.

Mawley is puzzled by Charles' anxiety over the letter that is waiting for him and, when it turns out to be from Penworth, by his indifference. In the book's closing sentence the melancholy, as Mawley sees it, of the late summer afternoon, is translated to Charles: 'Mawley, on looking up, observed that instead of unpacking he had remained sitting on the edge of his bed, his face expressionless like that of one who thinks steadfastly of something past and irrevocable, upon which great happiness had once depended.'

There is sadness here, and a poignant sense of loss, but none of the anger and aggrieved self-pity of the Lindsay letter.

The Young Desire It is a miracle, not least in that its wholeness, its freshness and clarity, seem magically untouched by the damage that casts such a shadow over Mackenzie's later years. Among Australian novels it is unique and very nearly perfect, a hymn to youth, to life, to sexual freedom and moral independence, written in full awareness – and this is its second miracle – of the cost, both to others and to oneself.

Introduction to The Young Desire It, *Text, 2013*

LES MURRAY: *LUNCH AND COUNTER LUNCH*

LES MURRAY IS PERHAPS the most naturally gifted poet of his generation in Australia, and *Lunch and Counter Lunch*, his fourth collection, contains some of his best work to date. Why, one wonders, have reviewers been unwilling to engage with the book on the serious terms it so obviously demands?

It is a work of astonishing dexterity and scope. The verbal inventiveness seems almost unlimited and one is reminded of late Auden in the poet's capacity to talk about almost anything and make it sizzle and twang. Murray never falls into easy attitudes and never gives shape to a 'received idea'. We are aware on every page of the freshness and originality of his insights, whether he is evoking landscape:

Out here, the trees
grow cooly under the earth

and the bush is branches

or making delicate observations about people.

> we are leaving the parts where Please and Excuse Me
>   are said
> the man up front of me
> hands his wife to one side as gently as crockery.

He has genuine wit, and what is rarer, genuine humour – some of it passionately black. The poems come in a stunning variety of modes: from the bush anecdote that is never mere anecdote ('Folklore', 'Sergeant Forby Lectures the Cadets'), through the Bly-like lyricism of 'Cycling in the Lake District', to big talky poems like 'The Action'. There is also, in the 'Broad Bean Sermon', with its evocation of the richness, the plurality, the oddness of the natural world, a marvellous paean of praise to the fulness of things – one of Murray's surest expressions of his religious vision – and in 'The Edge of the Forest' a return to the world of 'Evening Alone at Bunyah' that makes us understand from inside the humanity of a situation that might seem too ordinary for poetry. And the same is true, I think, of the best poem in the book, the policeman's monologue 'The Breach', which not only makes poetry out of the plainest speech but takes us movingly inside one man's dedication to duty, and opens, with no sense of strain, into a larger subject, the problem of humanising the law. There are, of course, moments of uneasy mannerism – they are the weakness of Murray's considerable strengths: as when what ordinary Australians call an Esky makes its appearance as 'a styrofoam box with a handle' and when the wit takes the form of terrible puns: 'the shirt of nexus'. But these are small defects and *Lunch and Counter Lunch* is a big book.

Les Murray's general stance, as commentators have already noted, is conservative, and this is challenging enough to need some comment.

Most of these poems are straightforwardly Christian: 'Say the law's a regent till the king comes back / if he does come.' They are also about such unfashionable subjects as nationhood, the need for law and order, the blood tie with land, and the manly virtues: 'Defaming the high words – honour, courage / has not stopped us. It has made us mad.'

The book is meant to make us uncomfortable. It is the work of a highly intelligent man who distrusts our modern intelligence and whose preferred faculties, one guesses, would be intuition, psychic vision, but also the countryman's plain commonsense and even plainer sense of decency. What I mean is that if what we have here is a conservative mind, it is a very critical and complex and flexible one – and given the current climate, to be a conservative as Murray is might be the most way-out form of radicalism. There is in these poems a feeling of going hard against the tide. It is what gives them their strong sense of energy, but also, I think, their edgy, aggressive/defensive tone.

So then, what is the trouble?

Quite early on in *Lunch and Counter Lunch* there is an important clue to what Murray is doing in this book. The poem is called 'L'esprit de l'escalier' and the line I am thinking of is: 'the perfect reply you only thought of later'. *Lunch and Counter Lunch* is full of perfect rejoinders, brilliant refutations of fashionable opinion, and one guesses that 'Argument and Counter Argument' lies somewhere behind the book's throw-away title.

The police poems, for example, in examining the problems of law and order, speak up strongly, in human terms, for its agents ('I am a policeman / it is easier to make me seem an oaf / than to handle the truth') and have as well some ironic observations to make about more 'progressive' attitudes: 'Reading modern stuff at times / you'd think all crime was protest, or illusion – / we should charge the victims'. 'The Action' seeks to humanise the world of change; it is a poem against historical necessity. 'Sidere Mens Eadem Mutato' while beautifully evoking the poet's student youth in the late fifties, questions the importance now accorded to the university as a seeding-ground for a new class, the intellectual élite, and a new and more brutally conformist culture, where, as Murray has it, 'Freud and Marx are left and right thongs in a goosestep'. 'Aqualung Shinto', on the whole the least attractive poem in the book, opts for the 'one entirely native/ the wisest Japanese faith' of the poem's title rather than the more fashionable Zen: *'We're all mystic intellectuals now* Don nodded. *But we were meant for soldiers.'* 'Portrait of the Autist As a New World Driver' mounts a moving defence of the automobile at the very moment when it is generally being presented as an ecological and economic monster – though as always the attitude behind the defence is complex: 'of course we love our shells: they make the ant-heap/ bearable of course the price is blood'. Murray's general lightness of touch, and the subtle sense of paradox, is nowhere better exemplified than in the turn into that last line.

What I find worrying in all this is not the attitudes – Murray is on the whole more caring, more human, than his antagonists – but the fact that in being replies, however brilliant, they have their source outside the poet: they are points in a public debate, they belong to the world of opinion, assertion, controversy; they spring, one wants to say, from the world of journalism and have the shape, and sometimes even the tone, of a newspaper column by a journalist who always takes an opposing line and largely relies on the exploitation of his own public personality. It is the tone I find most worrying of all. It is too often preachily rhetorical and condescending, too pleased with its own cleverness; and it results too often in a sort of dumpy deadness in the rhythm. But in objecting to what I have called the tone I am really objecting to something further back in the poem's conception that creates the tone.

For all its surprising twists and turns, Murray's creative intelligence doesn't seem quite free in this book. In making his 'brilliant replies' he has, in many ways, accepted limits that are posed for him, by assertions from 'out there'. *Lunch and Counter Lunch* strikes me as the work of a poet who is, at the midpoint of his career, very much in search of a subject that will be fully expressive of his gifts.

In earlier books one had the feeling that Murray's subjects were *found* – and so close at hand that he had merely to reach out and give them shape. The subjects in *Lunch and Counter Lunch* seem taken up, and they are, to this extent, gratuitous, vehicles for the intelligence and verbal flair of a man who can write well on anything. Only very occasionally do they have that ring of the personal that we associate with the best poetry: notably here in 'The Edge of the Forest' and more darkly in 'Rostered Duty'.

What is also clear is that the earlier material is now exhausted. There is no way back. 'Their Cities, Their Universities', despite some striking details, is for me one of Murray's least convincing performances. What was easy in the earlier poems is mannered, almost baroque here, the energy seems worked up. And this despite a conclusion that is one of the best things in the book: 'we are going to the cause / not coming from it'.

There is no doubt about Murray's stature. He is a powerful poet, with all the gifts, one might want to assert, of a potentially great one. This new book reveals him at a point of crisis. Whichever way he now turns, it will be the key work in his career.

Poetry Australia, *1974*

THE BOOK OF SAINTS: PATRICK WHITE'S *RIDERS IN THE CHARIOT*

IN APRIL 1958, SHORTLY after the appearance of *Voss*, Patrick White published a non-fiction piece in a new journal, *Australian Letters*.

Ten years earlier, after more than two decades away, he had returned with his partner, Manoly Lascaris, to the world of his Australian childhood and 'the stimulation' as he hoped 'of time remembered'. He *had* been stimulated, wonderfully so, *The Tree of Man* (1955) and *Voss* (1957) attest to that, but what 'The Prodigal Son' attests to is his bitter disappointment with the country to which, like a latter-day convict, he felt he had been 'transported', and 'for life'.

In all directions stretched the Great Australian Emptiness, in which the mind is the least of possessions, in which the rich man is the important man, in which the schoolmaster and the journalist rule what intellectual roost there is, in which beautiful youths and girls stare at life through blind blue eyes, in which teeth fall like autumn leaves, the buttocks of cars grow hourly glassier, food means steak and cake, muscles prevail, and the march of material ugliness does not raise a quiver from the average nerves. It was the exaltation of the 'average' that made me panic . . .

In 1964, James Stern, the most enthusiastic of White's American reviewers, wrote to him expressing disappointment at what seemed a move away from the larger vision of the earlier books towards something darker and more angrily judgemental. White defended himself:

Unfortunately we live in black times, with less and less that may be called good. I must reflect on the blackness of those times. I tried to write a book about saints, but saints are few and far between. If I were a saint myself I could project my saintliness, perhaps, endlessly in what I write. But I am a sensual and irritable human being. Certainly the longer I live the less I see I like in human beings of whom I am one.

The 'book of saints' was *Riders in the Chariot*, the third of the novels of his return and the first to deal with a contemporary Australia of mass migration and post-war boom. The book marks a new form of engagement in his work and much of what he lists in 'The Prodigal Son' finds a place there.

Set at Castle Hill (Sarsaparilla, White calls it) on the outskirts of Sydney, it chronicles the lives of four characters who, like most Australians, find themselves by an accident of fate in unlikely contact with one another: Mordecai Himmelfarb, a scholar of the Jewish mystics and an Auschwitz survivor, 'the blackfellow, or half-caste' painter, Alf Dubbo, that 'angel of solid light' the English migrant and evangelical washerwoman, Ruth Godbold, and the owner of Xanadu, and last offshoot of a ruined colonial family, mad Miss Hare. What these characters have in common is that they have all known 'ecstasy' and are members of the small band of the just who in each generation are the redeemers of the earth.

Ranged against them in the novel are the upholders of the 'average' at Sarsaparilla: Mrs Flack, Mrs Jolley, whose blue eyes 'see just so far and no farther', and that beautiful torso and spoiled, toothless head – the 'Antinoüs of the suburbs' White calls him – Mrs Flack's nephew, Blue, who fills the role of Himmelfarb's young tormentor at Rosetree's Brighta Bicycle Lamps workshop at Barranugli (White's way with cod aboriginal place names is typical of his sometimes broad humour), and the instigator, at the climax of the novel, of his 'crucifixion'.

White had set out in his two previous novels to

uncover 'the mystery and poetry which alone', he feels, 'can make bearable the lives of ordinary men and women', but also to replace with a rich inwardness the obsession with material possessions – 'the texture-brick home, the streamlined glass car, the advanced shrubs, the grandfather clock with the Westminster chimes, the walnut-veneer radiogram, the washing-machine, and the Mixmaster' – with which the Rosetrees and others, out of terminal anxiety at their own emptiness and inauthenticity, fill the void of their days. He had also written in 'The Prodigal Son' of his determination to show that the Australian novel 'is not necessarily the dreary, dun-coloured offspring of journalistic realism' – or, he might have added, considering his immediate contemporaries, of rose-coloured Socialist Realism. 'I would like,' he writes, 'to give my book the textures of music, the sensuousness of paint.'

Of all White's novels, *Riders* is the one that most aspires to the condition of music – its interweaving voices barely connect at the level of the actual – but it also aspires to the condition of theatre. In the eighteen months after its completion White produced three plays, two of them set, like the novel, in Sarsaparilla and its surroundings.

White had always been drawn to the theatre, and especially to the revue, that very British mix of satire, comic turns and sometimes outrageous camp. *Riders*, in the emblematic names of its characters, in the

choric voice of Sarsaparilla – the voice of 'native cynicism' and 'derision' as it is embodied in Mrs Jolley and
Mrs Flack – has more than a little of the old morality
play, where high spiritual drama is intermingled, as
here, with slapstick or burlesque. Even Himmelfarb,
under direction of his 'fate', sees the Seder table he has
prepared for Passover as so much a 'property table'
that 'it would not have been illogical if, in the course
of the farce he was elaborating, a *Hanswurst* had risen
through the floor'. His Bosch-like crucifixion when it
comes is suggested to his tormentors by the passing of
a circus parade, in which a clown, a Petrushka in fact,
goes through a mock hanging: 'Those who had longed
for a show wondered whether they were appeased, for
the clown was surely more or less a puppet, when they
had been hoping for a man.'

The mock crucifixion that follows is passed off by the
factory foreman, Ernie Theobalds, as good-humoured
horseplay, larrikin high spirits, but Himmelfarb recognises it at once for what it is: the same mob fury and
resentment of what is different that is behind every
pogrom or massacre or ritual killing. He has rejected
the real Promised Land only to find himself in a less
promising one where carnivalesque misrule appears
as mere loutishness, and 'history' is regularly reenacted
as farce.

White, here as elsewhere, is at his most characteristic when the noble and the shameful are in violent

but comic collision. In Himmelfarb's appearance, an unwelcome Elijah, at the Rosetrees' Seder, or the Dostoevskian scene at Mrs Khalil's where, while an outraged Mr Hoggett waits for one of the 'juicy' Khalil girls to become available, Mrs Godbold ministers to a drunken Alf Dubbo. It is on this occasion that Ruth Godbold's capacity for forgiveness – White is merciless here – becomes more at last than her husband, Tom, can bear. Most extraordinary of all is the travesty of the four riders that Mrs Jolley and Mrs Flack present as they 'drench the room in the moth-colours of their one mind', which would have been 'the perfect communion of souls, if, at the same time, it had not suggested perfect collusion'.

Mrs Jolley, bearer of 'the virtues' to Xanadu, protectress of the home and the Hoover, for whom 'all was sanctified by cake', is one of the great comic monsters of modern fiction.

Introduced 'feeling the way with her teeth', and with a voice with 'the clang' of a Melbourne tram in it, she shares something – her ferocious propriety but also perhaps her literary past as a Panto Dame – with Barry Humphries' Edna Everage (Average) when she was still just a Melbourne matron; that is, before she had become, in rivalry with Joan Sutherland ('La Stupenda'), Dame Edna Superstar. Verbally, Mrs Jolley is created almost exclusively in terms of the material objects she so passionately believes in.

White's language world is full of the capacity of objects to transmute and fetishise themselves as aspects of the human. It is what gives such vivid and disturbing life to the writing, and a fantastic and sometimes lurid quality to its most ordinary moments. It is also what creates the poetry of occasions when what might otherwise be inexpressible is made wonderfully substantial to us 'in all the sensuousness of paint'. When the plum tree, for example, under which Miss Hare goes through her mystic marriage with Himmelfarb, becomes an oriental canopy where shadows lie 'curled like heavy animals, spotted and striped with tawny light', or 'the 'ball of friendship' that appears as a 'golden sphere' that hangs briefly, 'lovely and luminous to see', between Himmelfarb and Mrs Godbold.

If Himmelfarb's pre-war life, *tour de force* though it is, seems a little stiff in the narration, too panoramic in movement, and in detail too phantasmagoric to be more than sketchily there, it is because the rest is so dense with observed detail, so full of what Mrs Godbold sees as 'the commotion of life' – though one should add that the train-journey to Auschwitz, and the unforgettable Lady from Czernowitz, are among the finest things White was ever to write. Early in the book Miss Hare worries that 'so many of the things she told died on coming to the surface, when their life, to say nothing of their after life in her mind, could be such a shining one'.

How to communicate what they have seen without killing it in the telling is a torment to a good many of White's characters, even those who see nothing much. It is what drives some of them to violence.

White too puts more value on what is inexpressible than on what can too easily be expressed, but what he brings to the surface does shine. There are whole pages here that, once they have become part of what he has made visible to us, once we have experienced them through the texture of his peculiar music, live on in our mind as if they had been our own shining experience to tell.

Towards the end of *Riders,* White delivers one of his most savage sermons on the ugly, character-less fibro homes that have replaced the grand folly of Xanadu. Two pages later, in the beautiful coda to the book, Mrs Godbold looks at these same houses and, with her 'very centre . . . touched by the wings of love and charity', sees something quite different.

> Mrs Godbold could not help admiring the houses for their signs of life: for the children coming home from school, for a row of young cauliflowers, for a convalescent woman, who had stepped outside in her dressing gown to gather a late rose.

Only the greatest masters can stand aside and allow themselves to be admonished by one of their creations, whose vision, by some miracle of autonomy, is larger than their own.

Introduction to Riders in the Chariot,
New York Review Books, 2002

CHRISTINA STEAD AT EIGHTY

I FIRST READ *For Love Alone*, the Stead novel that deals directly with her Australian experience, twelve years ago. Like so many of her books it begins as a fairytale (she is essentially a teller of tales – monstrous ones) but soon becomes the richest picture we have of an Australian family and of the making within it of an individual sensibility – the more striking for its being, in this case, that of a passionate and courageous girl. Teresa Hawkins has a strong sense of personal honour ('I would kill anyone who offends my honour,' she says, and means by that just what a man would mean) and is determined, in the face of poverty, provincialism and a charming but selfish father who lives off the attention of females, to find a full life for herself, somewhere and with someone. This being a Stead novel, she does.

For Love Alone was not written early and it was not written here. It shows the effect of distance. The narrative is crowded, precise and sensuous, but the writer is not mesmerised by her earlier self or by the place where she began. She is not limited by being either a woman or an Australian.

Stead has a woman's wry and sometimes angry knowledge of the sex-war – which doesn't look like a war – but she expresses it like a writer. Her most destructive male characters are full of weakness and charm (Tom Cotter) as well as selfish chauvinism (Sam Pollit, Robert Grant), and some of her subtlest monsters are women. She takes it for granted that a woman may be an active agency, just like a man. We must be grateful to the feminists for having quite properly taken her up, but we do not need to think of her as a feminist writer, or worse, a woman writer. She has the kind of toughness, intelligence, interest in how things *work* (no-one understands better the world of banking, investment, shabby back-street dealing) of the born novelist – a category in which sex is important but gender is not.

Nor does she belong, essentially, to Australian literature. The four books at the centre of her achievement deal with 'the matter of America'. They are a passionate critique of its failed idealisms (*The People with the Dogs*), and of the various forms of cannibalism (*A Little Tea, A Little Chat*) of its capitalist mode. The streets of New York, the Washington area of *The Man Who Loved Children*, the Catskills,

Virginia in full summer, all these are created with the same density and precise feeling for place and creature as the harbourside of *For Love Alone*. And when Stead shifts to England, she creates in *Cotter's England* a sombre, coal-black account of one 'dark place of the heart', of the miseries of poverty, of helpless or crazy old age, of youth betrayed and betraying, that seems at this distance unequalled among the English novels of its decade for the acuteness of its home truths.

She writes about where she is. She belongs wherever she puts down her intelligence and allows it to take root.

Her forte is the making of monsters. They are monsters of egotism whose energy is terrible; they never stop talking, they never sit still. Brilliant, self-deceiving, wheedling, sentimental, funny talk comes tumbling out of their mouths; it is a web to catch others with its charm; it smothers and consumes them. It is a form of power.

The power-game begins at home. Brothers and sisters, parents and children, tear one another apart; they love, feed, tyrannise over one another; they eat each other up.

The alternative to the *actual* family is the made one – those households that proliferate in these books as havens for the odd and disorderly, like Edward's house off 14th Street, or the one at Scratch Park in *The People with the Dogs*, or Nellie's refuge for women in *Cotter's England*. Even here, the exploitation, the slaughter, goes on. It is Stead's political vision that allows her to move with such authority between worlds, from private to public, from one part of the system to another; to Europe (*House of All Nations*), to England, to America, then back again. The political vision is also the moral one. 'Satan,' as Oneida Massine ironically puts it in *The People with the Dogs*, 'finds work for busy hands.'

As so often in the blacker comedies, the villains have all the energy and charm. Evil knows what it wants, and goes on, out of sheer animal vitality as well as lust or greed, to get it. The spectacle is both horrible and marvellous.

It is Stead's image of America – American idealism, American capitalism as the poles of the system – that stands at the centre of her work. The view is dark. Only the 'fiftieth state', the Massine enclave at Whitehouse, offers any hope, and Edward, the hero of *The People with the Dogs*, has to escape it to find a life of his own. Still, he recognises the achievement:

With a little goodwill and mutual aid and sensible nonchalance, with live and let live, we can take vacations from the epoch of wars and revolutions.

Vacations. The Massines' is a holiday world of 'creative sloth'. It doesn't keep the farm going, but it is there. Even the crazy airman Bart has to salute the 'comedians on the hill'. 'You might,' he tells them, 'be the last people alive. You would not be a bad crowd to start the human race again.'

Angry, passionate, loving, tolerant, fascinated by the richness of things natural, things made, by talk, jokes, deals of every sort, and the energy of even the most vicious creatures in her aquarium, Christina Stead has the scope, the imagination, the objectivity of the greatest novelists.

With characteristic generosity Patrick White recognised this when he chose her for the first of his Nobel Prize awards. She is his great contemporary. They are an awesome pair. We are lucky, we readers, to have both of them.

Sydney Morning Herald,
Saturday 17 July 1982

SCINTILLATING STEAD

THERE IS A MOMENT towards the end of *The People with the Dogs*, the last of Christina Stead's American novels, when we are offered the nearest thing we get in her world to a moment of achieved harmony. The scene is a wedding feast:

At that moment the family, not specially arranged, but in a natural order, stood about at the door, in the lobby, and on the two flights of stairs, as well as in the room, and round the table, waiting for the toasts. There was no silence or constraint, no impatience and no flurry. In this moment, as in all others, their long habit and innocent, unquestioning and strong, binding family love, the rule of their family, made all things natural and sociable with them.

The Massines here are the ideal community. Families in these novels, those earliest models of the sociable, are not always so innocent, their rule is seldom so easy and without constraint; and those two terms, 'natural' and 'sociable', that seem here like two aspects of the same achievement, are more often in a warring relationship on opposite sides.

From the beginning Christina Stead has been a novelist of communal and sociable man, of action and the crowded life of cities. Her first work, *Seven Poor Men of Sydney*, is already a city novel, dealing with intellectuals, radicals, people of mind and soul trying to make their way under the pressure of hard economic conditions, aspiring to life and love in 'modern times'. With no other novelist I know (except Balzac) are we so aware always of where work and money belong in the characters' lives. And yet they are not simply the product of their environment. Letty Fox is an absolutely modern woman, a New Yorker to her fingertips. 'To be plain,' she tells us, 'I despised the country and only used it to grow up in. Like plants and sheep.' She is at home only in the fast-moving eat-or-be-eaten world of the city; she is utterly socialised. Yet she recognises the force that has her cousin Cecily in its grip as something anterior to society and its rules, as something primeval and darkly mysterious:

She loved the night. She slept out on the grass. One summer night we saw her walking naked between the garage and the house. The sky was bright with stars. This seemed awful to us, and Cecily was clothed for us in mystery and danger from that night on.

*

Cecily is a key figure in *Letty Fox, Her Luck*. Responsive to nature and its forces, and endowed with a rich and precocious sexuality, she wants, at twelve, to be married to her boy Carl, but is mocked and frustrated by those for whom sexuality belongs not to 'nature' but to the rules and regulations made by men. She is driven to suicide. Another cousin, Elvira, equally precocious, has her photograph taken in the nude and distributed to admirers. Sex for her is already something that belongs in the world of advertising, to commerce. She follows the rules.

There is a sense in which, if we are to see our lives as having some other shape than a string of random events, we must read them as 'stories', using, as dreams do, the oldest and most primitive forms we know, the folk-tale and fairy story.

Christina Stead is a born teller of tales as well as a sharp and scientific observer of creatures in an environment. Even the most modern of her novels, the most firmly rooted in economic reality, have the shape

282

of fairy stories and are in touch with the world from which they derive. This, in the end, is what seems rarest and most original in her. Her characters belong to society and are determined by it, but they also see themselves as belonging to a world in which what is being acted out are fables older than society and more deeply connected to what is human. Even that hard-headed modern miss, Letty Marmalade (always in a jam), has to go twice into the house of the witch, Lucy Headlong, to 'the sacred mount, the haunted grove' and suffer fierce ordeals of body and spirit ('I thought of things in legend, the shirt burning like fire, the potions, the brews, the love-draughts') before she is ready to meet her Prince Charming, a real millionaire no less; though it is in the nature of Letty's luck, and of this modern fairytale, that he should by the time she marries him be a millionaire only in name. Characters here suddenly act in ways that take them right out of modern times, and the satirical mode, into something more like the world of the Brothers Grimm; as when Percy Hogg, of *Letty Fox*, meets the boys who have escaped from the prison farm and steals their stolen meat:

Hogg, to conceal his wild exultation at having eaten the stolen meat, stopped to gather a mandrake he saw. He carefully loosened the soil and brought up the strange plant . . .

However accurately placed and defined by the society they find themselves in, these characters do not have their whole being there; neither do the books. It is what makes the tone of Christina Stead's writing so complex and ambiguous and the works so difficult to categorise. They escape – they marvellously escape – all the usual modes.

Letty Fox, as its narrator tells us, is 'a book of a girl's life. Men don't like to think that we are just as they are; but we are . . .'. She means by this that a woman can be an active agency with her own fate and her own object in life. Letty's object may seem to be that of any romantic heroine: 'My supreme idea was always to get married and join organised society . . . I like to be decent; and in the table of decency a husband comes before anything else'; but her situation is not at all that of the romantic heroine.

'In other times,' she tells us, 'society regarded us as cattle or handsome house slaves; the ability to sell ourselves in any way we like is a step towards freedom.'

The wry irony of that 'freedom' is at the heart of the book and of Letty's hard-headed acceptance of limitations. This is the book of Letty Fox's '*Education Sentimentale*', at the hands of many men – most of them weak, self-regarding, sentimental, hypocritical exploiters of women in Stead's most assured manner – and a whole tribe of women: her timid mother, Mathilde (awful example of the downtrodden and rejected wife), Granny Fox, Granny Morgan, the terrible Dora Morgan, and various girlfriends: Hilda, Pauline, and that expert on the subject, the maverick Australian Amy, whose findings are presented in the form of a jokey (but deadly serious) catechism:

Q.: I love my fiancé, but I love another man, too – what shall I do?

A.: Throw up a nickel. If it comes down heads, stick to your fiancé; if it comes down tails, stick to your fiancé.

Q.: What about a girl most attracts a man?

A.: Other men.

Q.: But how can you hold a man?

A.: If there were any known way we wouldn't have marriage laws.

Q.: I'm taller than he is; I'm embarrassed when we're walking down the street. What can I do?

A.: Walk in the gutter while he walks on the kerb; or let him take you about in a wheelchair.

Q.: He doesn't respect me now that we've slept together.

A.: Then it's a good thing you didn't marry him.

Q.: I love him but he doesn't make enough to live on.

A.: Marry someone else.

Amy's wickedly accurate analysis of the relations between the sexes is dramatised in the book's wide range of encounters and confrontations.

Money is of the essence. It frequently replaces some other factor in a well-known formula. 'He held my knee and showed me his wallet,' Letty's silly mother says of Mr Montrose; and another family friend, Mr McLaren, gives Letty's father some early advice on child-raising:

A child starts off with the right idea of society if she has a little of her own, and I'm sorry you have let the first two years pass without her owning something. Thus, two years have passed during which she belonged to the underdogs, and I'm sorry to observe that this has a bad effect on the character and temper in our class of society . . . Let me have a child during the first seven dollars and I can guarantee its success afterwards.

When Letty does have a little of her own, Granny Fox's $2500, its gradual whittling away provides one of the book's chief plot interests. Men are deeply attracted by it. 'I attracted men enough,' Letty tells us, 'but I could not,' she adds, with wry ambiguity, 'keep them.' Her sister Jacky fares even worse. 'Oh, I have boyfriends,' she tells Letty. 'One of them wanted to marry me. He wrote mother a letter. He asked her in the same letter if the $2500 would be paid at once and if mother's piano would go along with me.'

Such is the world Letty works and uses her freedom

in, the world in which she has to save her life, find a man – 'a man, not half a human couple' – and have her children.

The crown of all this is the 'alimony game', that specifically American addition to the war between the sexes; especially in the new and improved form in which it is practised by the second Mrs Bosper. The French Canadian Pauline, brought up on European manners, offers the sharpest view of it:

What luck you have, you American women! Men who pay for everything and don't ask for accounts. Yes, it's Protestantism. The men believe they've done their women an insult and injury by sleeping with them. They must pay for ever . . . Oh Golconda of women! And then, one's not obliged to stay with one man. Not at all. A woman can try one man after another and each one's obliged to pay for the privilege of sleeping with her, but only, of course, when he has stopped sleeping with her; it's sleep with, or go to jail for alimony.

Percy Hogg and Philip Morgan, Letty's uncles, both go to jail for alimony, and Philip, another tragic victim like Cecily, who cannot reconcile sexuality to the laws of the land, hangs himself outside Letty's bathroom window.

The system is monstrously unnatural and cruel to both sexes. To survive and stay human, as Letty does, and to have a real life, is no easy matter. Letty does it by being 'wide-awake' and on all occasions honest with herself; by knowing the rules of the game and playing them to the letter and beyond, but without cruelty or vindictiveness; by having, as she puts it, 'principles, even in a really evil setting'; and by having *luck*.

Two more of Amy's questions and answers need quoting:

Q.: But do you think I'll get a man if I stick to all this?
A.: You'll get one anyway.
Q.: Isn't this mere intrigue, trickery, unsuitable for a decent girl?
A.: Success is crime.

Letty is simply as kind, good, honest, natural and free as her world allows her to be.

*

'Success is crime' might have done very well as the epigraph of *A Little Tea, A Little Chat*. It is the most blackly comic of Christina Stead's masterpieces. The opening sets the tone and suggests something of its cold, clear, objective view of things:

Peter Hoag, a Wall Street man, aged 56 in March, 1941, led a simple Manhattan life and had regular habits. He lived alone in a furnished apartment at $110 monthly, on the 18th floor of a residential hotel in the lower East Sixties . . . The people below looked so small that they seemed like two-legged fleas, and the cars so small that they were like potato-bugs that could be scooped up by the hatful.

A latter-day City Comedy, full of coney-catching devices of the most resourceful and up-to-date sort, and over-reachers of all kinds and both sexes, *A Little Tea* has at its centre a comic character of Volpone-like dimensions.

Robert Grant is devoted to the double art of seduction and swindling; for him woman and commodities are indistinguishable. 'Property is a woman,' he tells his son, Gilbert, in an extraordinary eight-page lecture on the morality of money; and the two become one in Stead's definition of sexual gambits:

He did not care for the pursuit, nor for adventure. Ever since his early manhood, since his marriage, he had bought women; most had been bargains and most had made delivery at once. He never paid in advance: 'I got no time for futures in women.'

Grant's world is a world of deals both big and small, of exploitation, dog-eat-dog betrayals, of snooping, spying, anonymous letters and saleable secrets. Grant cannot stop talking, cannot sit still, and never has his hand out of someone's pocket. Stead marvellously catches the style in which he 'gives himself away', a style that is meant to confuse as well as fascinate:

> He dropped clues, lifted masks, showed his tracks, all through his discourse, and then seeing what he had done, doubled back on himself, made false scents, artfully mixed in incompatibles, but not with any true idea of dodging them, but of keeping their minds intent on himself and his romantic situation. He did not care what they saw as long as they kept looking and wondering at him. He felt all kinds of rich emotions, a sentimental innocence in the pleasure of showing himself to them as a creature they had never dreamed of – more sorrowful, wickeder, gayer, more romantic, more lecherous, more bewildered.

Grant's twists and turns, his rapid shifts of pace, focus, object are like Stead's own; the book lives off Grant's energy which is a law unto itself, a force of nature. Garrulous, mean, obsessive, self-parodying, Grant also has great charm and in the end – and this is one of the book's major achievements – real pathos. He is a comic monster who out-natures nature and breaks free of any attempt his creator might make to place him morally. He longs to have his life turned into a Broadway hit, and his attempt to achieve this in

partnership with a crazy dramatist 'of European reputation' is one of the most comic things in the book; but
like Volpone, or Brecht's Pierpont Mauler, he is too
big for the drama he is in already; his energy cannot
contain itself or be contained. He cheats without
discrimination because it is his 'nature'. He takes his
profit everywhere. When he is given an apartment to
hide in, which he soon sublets, 'he began peering into
cupboards. He found salt, coffee and canned milk
in the kitchen – a profit. In one of the drawers was a
small enamelled pill-case about one inch square. He
liked this and pocketed it.' His passion for boxes of all
sorts, and for keys to open and close them, is fetish-
istic, an unexplained 'humor' that produces some
of the book's zaniest conversations and scenes. His
excuse always is that he is a creature of the society
that produced him:

'If I'd been born in a land where they wouldn't let me
put my hand in your pocket – not yours, Edda – I'd
be a good commissar. But I'm corrupted. I'm a profi-
teer. Will I stand by and let others take the pickings?
It's asking too much . . . When the golden harvest has
begun, take a scythe in your hand . . .'

His undoing is the Blondine, in her various disguises
as Mrs Downs or Mrs Kent, and the 'Great Blond
Network'. She destroys him because she is a creature

of his own kind ('I go into the daily battle with men,' she tells the son, Gilbert, 'I meet them on their own terms . . . I do exactly what your father does'); but Grant is also a victim of his own 'sentimental innocence':

> '– I should not say this, but perhaps I was not always as I should have been, but without any thought of harm, I swear, I was carried away. I saw her, by lamplight, on the fresh linen, with her blond hair uncoiled and a white cat there, a picture of innocence asleep, with a rosy cheek and hardly breathing, like that princess, the Sleeping Beauty, I kissed her forehead and up there woke a rascal and a criminal.'

Our last view of the terrible pair is utterly banal: a parody Darby and Joan, suspicious, dependent, resentful of one another, still dashing off the occasional poison-pen letter. Abruptly the Brechtian farce, the 'exemplary comedy', opens up to let in a figure from quite another world, the world of folk-tale or nightmare, the mysterious Hilburtson ('Gilbert' the Negro maid calls him, in some obscure but disturbing confusion with Grant's son) who steps out of Grant's past, or out of his shadow, in the shape of an old, white-headed caller – Death as Grant has already imagined him – to strike the man down.

It's a splendid and terrifying conclusion. Mere

farce in the end, mere satire or morality play, could not contain Grant or properly finish him off. His end belongs to some darker genre. He is a creation of the highest imaginative order, all energy without object, replacing nature with talk, with deals, with breathless activity, but at the centre empty; when the bubble bursts there is nothing there. It is, fully dramatised and without comment, a critique both of the 'creature' and of the society that made him.

*

'Satan', says Oneida, the youngest and liveliest of the Massine women of *The People with the Dogs*, 'finds work for busy hands is what I see. People who can't keep still are soon at work poisoning or throttling – or slaughtering each other.'

She might be thinking of Robert Grant, though there is no possibility of her meeting him in this novel. The world she inhabits, the book, stands at the farthest possible point from *A Little Tea, A Little Chat*, though both deal with the same city. It is a question of tone. *The People with the Dogs* discovers in New York itself, and in the country upstate, another mode of social and communal existence than the cannibalistic one we see so savagely depicted in Grant's book, or the frenetic rat-race of *Letty Fox*.

The centre of all this is the extended family of the

Massines, 'the Comedians on the Hill' with 'their wedding guests, their bride and groom, and Irene, Edward, Lou and "the morons"' – they are wonderfully inclusive with their cult of 'creative sloth' as justified by Oneida's reversal of the adage that is the basis of the Protestant work ethic; and Whitehouse, 'the Massine enclave' – the 'Fiftieth State of the Union' – established by old Dad Massine 'with the following sweet words: "I leave you Whitehouse to furnish a roof for you all, rich, poor, working, idle. All will be free on the Home Farm to do as they like . . ."'

*

Edward, the hero of the book, the soldier home from the wars, whose slow passage towards marriage makes up what there is of a plot, salutes the rareness of what Whitehouse and the clan have achieved, while recognising that he has to escape it to make a life of his own: '"I can't bear to see the Massine Republic change," he says, with tears in his eyes . . . "Will you change the Republic of Arts and Letters and Human Sloth? Why there, with a little good will and mutual aid and sensible mild nonchalance, with live and let live, we take vacations from the epoch of wars and revolutions. Oh, keep Musty away. My soul! Must we be efficient too?"'

Musty is one of the many dogs who share this book with so many people. He is – in one of those allusions that playfully abound in the verbal texture of Christina Stead's writing – 'the dog that's friend to man', and his presence in Edward's fine effusion serves to qualify its absoluteness.

Whitehouse is an ideal, but is a place for 'vacations'. 'Creative sloth' does achieve something but it also lets the farm go to seed. Still, what Whitehouse and the Massines offer is the nearest thing we have in Christina Stead's world to a society devoted to 'all things natural and sociable', untorn by the other instincts of personal cruelty, political tyranny and greed.

The family and its 'innocent, unquestioning and strong, binding family love' is one centre of it. The other is the loosely formed alternative 'households' of the book, Edward's off Stuyvesant Park, the Christy refuge at Scratch Park, 'chosen' families of the odd, the lonely, the disaffected, the independent, the aimless, and those who simply want to be free for a little of other ties.

'Imagine being born into your own company,' says the actress Lydia, Edward's future wife, 'I have to recruit mine.' Company here replaces the usual word, society, and enters the book free from any 'business' association, as a term describing, in the special light of this one novel, an association of free individuals in a spirit of play.

The People with the Dogs is itself, within Stead's opus, a kind of vacation book – a holiday from the darker view, an alternative, both as possibility and vision. There is death here: Phillip Christy dies under a trolley trying to save his dog; there is folly; there is also loving kindness. It is a book that celebrates American inclusiveness – people, animals, a rich profusion: 'old boxes and trunks and drawers overflowing with the possessions, goods, gifts that they had all showered on each other . . . big pieces of silk, brocades, exotic rugs, things that are in the order of the Massine family love'. This is the innocent side of possessiveness. It is a world devoted, after the American ideal, to brotherliness and the pursuit of happiness.

The People with the Dogs no more denies the vision of *A Little Tea, A Little Chat* than *A Winter's Tale* does the darker vision of *Timon*. It is the same world seen in a new light and re-created in a different mode. That Stead is able to do this – to step outside what might be seen as the necessity of her own vision – is part of her strength, her extraordinary intelligence and objectivity. The kind of novelist who can create, in such detail and with such force and conviction, two views of the same world that seem equally personal, equally necessary, but so different, is very rare indeed.

It is the diversity of these three books, each in its way a masterpiece, that most convinces us of her genius. She is, for some things, quite without equal among the makers of modern fiction.

The Age, *September 1982*

TIMON IN CENTENNIAL PARK

THE FINEST ACCOUNT I know of the artist's life (it too is an autobiography) is the *Memoirs* of Hector Berlioz. Rather in the manner of a novelist, Berlioz uses himself as the basis for a 'character', a posturing and passionately foolish Romantic, the victim of melancholy, genius, ill luck, bureaucracy, unrequited love and the envy of his less talented contemporaries, who just happens to have written the works ascribed to the composer of the same name. The character is a masterpiece. Superbly ironic and self-distancing, Berlioz has created an autobiographical self so convincing that his real self disappears, and he is free to do this because the work of a composer, in being abstract, has no visible continuity with his life; it does not draw for its material on real, verifiable experience.

The novelist who makes the same attempt is already compromised. Much of what he has to tell will already have found its way, transmuted in the light of inner weather and significantly deepened, into the fictions, and since so much experience is shared between the life and the work we expect to be shown the link between them.

We are mostly disappointed. The gap between the writer and the Writer is of the same kind as the gap between Berlioz as he appears in the *Memoirs* (or as he might have appeared in life) and the composer of *The Damnation of Faust*. All of which is to suggest that *Flaws in the Glass* is a book that tells us very little, save by implication, about the writer of *The Twyborn Affair* or *Voss*; about the man, that is, who sits at a desk and discovers himself in his fictions. *That* Patrick White we can know only through the novels, and the author of this self-portrait cannot tell us about him. *Flaws in the Glass* is in a different mode from the novels and comes from a different level of experience. It is written by the self White *knows*, and to this known self the author of the novels is a torment and a mystery:

I never re-read my books once I have corrected the proof, but if for some specific reason I have to open one and glance at a paragraph or two, I am struck by an element that must have got into them while I was under hypnosis. On one level certainly, there is a recognizable collage of personal experience, on another, little of the self I know. This unknown man is the man the interviewers, the visiting professors, the thesis writers expect to find, and because I am unable to produce him I have given up receiving them. I don't want to pretend to be me.

But if White cannot produce 'the author of the novels', who does he produce and what does *Flaws in the Glass* tell us about him?

He produces the sensitive, generous, vulnerable, impatient, autocratic, intolerantly opinionated *man* – the Patrick White whose life the novelist inhabits and to some extent shares: an Australian born in 1912 into the New South Wales squattocracy, educated abroad and for a time living there, in England, Spain, Germany, the United States, Egypt, Greece, growing up homosexual, moving with his generation into a war and into the inevitable disillusionments of the period we call 'after the war'. Because he is a great public figure, and has touched so much of the century, we are eager to hear what he has to say; but it is the man, the man in daily relationship with the world about him, who is the subject of this account: his relationship to his White and Withycombe aunts and uncles; to his mother, Ruth, and to Dicky Bird, his charming but ineffectual father; to the houses of his childhood and their moods and rituals; to the servants (especially Nurse Lizzie) who were his earliest loved-ones;

to Manoly, especially Manoly, since the other great interest of this book is its account of a marriage – in the event a lasting one – between the representatives of opposing but not quite incompatible cultures and the inheritors of different but complementary histories. It is the relationship with Manoly that gives the book its final shape, as it gives final shape also to the life.

The real centre of *Flaws in the Glass* is what might appear to the casual reader to be an afterthought, the section called 'Journeys', in which White uses his travels in Greece as a way of talking about his relationship to the Greek side of his own nature, which Manoly embodies and has led him to explore.

'Nobody writing a book on the Aegean Islands,' he tells us in a revealing glimpse into his method, 'would link those I'm about to include. They are dissimilar in character and from different groups, but each plays a particular role in my relationship with Greece and Manoly. Over and over, during these journeys and after, when M. tells me I hate Greece, I cannot explain my love. Again, in our more bitter, alcoholic arguments in the kitchen after the evening meal, when he tells me I hate *him*, I cannot prove that what I believe in most deeply, the novels for which my conscious self can't take full responsibility, our discomforting but exhilarating travels through Greece, our life together, its eruptions and rewards, my own clumsy wrestling with what I see as a religious faith – that all of this is what keeps me going.'

Greece is central to White. He has shared his life with a Greek, and taken on, in no way gratuitously or lightly, all the sufferings and resentments of the Greek diaspora. 'The Greek,' he writes, 'is never wholly unconscious of the echoes from a torture chamber in which his psyche is a present victim. Initiated into cruelty by Turk and German he is not above torturing his fellow Greek, which rebounds on him as self-torture.'

It is not only out of loyalty that White has embraced this version of what it is to be Greek. His sympathy with such modes of feeling predates the meeting with Manoly. His discovery of a pre-history for them gave shape to a predisposition and the vision that springs from it rather than calling it suddenly into existence.

No-one who has read the novels needs to be told that this vision is pessimistic. The pessimism expresses itself in *Flaws in the Glass* as black anger and a despair that is virtually unrelieved, but also has its comic side – 'We had arrived,' White tells us of their trip to Santorini, 'not yet the anti-climax' – and may seem the result, to some readers, not of a flaw in the universe but of the glass that has been held up to it; as much an aspect of the observer's impatience and ill-humour as of 'the nature of things'. This is one of the risks White runs in being truthful: 'What you truly feel about a country or an individual of great importance to you shocks you when you are honest about your feelings. If you are pure, innocent, or noble – qualities I don't lay claim to – perhaps you never develop passionate antipathies.'

It is also a risk that is inherent in the form. Pessimism here cannot transcend itself, as it does in the novels, by becoming the source of a view that is at once tragic and comic/grotesque; or through action that is blackly and piteously absurd.

In the novels too the sufferings meted out to the characters, the indignities they endure, may seem deliberately chosen by the author, but the texture of feeling is so convincing, and so deeply interwoven with events, that we accept the view as both whole and necessary: the creator takes responsibility for the world he has created. White is a stern god. He loves best those of his characters who are most tormented, those whom he has chosen to torment. 'Lacerations and visions' – a phrase used here of the Greek experience – comes close to defining the nature of his own experience of the world and the law of the world he creates; and it is significant that Greek, in this case, does not refer to the classical Greece of Plato and Sophocles, or even Aeschylus, but to the gaudy, decadent and god-obsessed 'matter of Byzantium' – or rather, the latter-day echo of it in the Smyrna Greeks, whose sufferings belong not to some remote and bloody corner of the Middle Ages but to living memory.

The Greek and the Australian worlds are in sharp contrast here. It is a long way from the experience of Dicky Bird and Ruth to the life Manoly's sisters are enduring in war-ravaged Athens, or from the world of the Withycombe Whites in 1922 to the contemporary expulsion from Smyrna. It is part of the book's purpose to show how White's life, through a series of fateful encounters, has come to accommodate both, and how, by opening his fiction to the whole of contemporary history he has been able to set it at the centre of a century's most violent extremes.

That is how the Greek/Australian connection works in the fiction. Here we see it at the level of daily living, through White's relationship with Manoly: 'Most Greeks cannot help but stroll, it is something to do with their legs and the nearness of the near east, while the majority of Anglo Saxons, especially Withycombes, march. So there is always a distance between us when Manoly and I go for a walk. No one else would see the invisible threads connecting us . . .'

Flaws in the Glass is about those invisible threads that connect a sturdy Anglo-Saxon on the march with all that White understands by 'Greek'; it is also about the threads that connect two selves; the writer to the man and personal experience to that other form of it that grows from the writing.

Since it is 'Patrick White' we are dealing with, it is the account of a life lived passionately in that hell to which the writer believes we are all condemned, and which the most truthful of us recognise; which is *this* world and all we can know of the next. The vision is existential. It is also – to use a term we associate with Swift and with Blake – excremental: 'the unsinkable condom and the smell of shit which precede the moment of illumination make it more rewarding when it happens'.

The individual who endures all this is stubborn, courageous, tormented, and as this book presents him – with his passionated hatred and grumpiness fully exposed – almost aggressively unlikeable. But the unlikeableness is not convincing.

If the flaws that are inherent in the glass prevent White from giving us an objective view of the world, they also prevent him from being objective about himself, and it is typical of the man, as of the writer, that in allowing for his own 'romanticism' he should choose to err on the side of ugliness in the one and a prickly irascibility in the other. There is evidence here of a warmer character than he cares to present. He has great loyalty and affection for those who have won his trust (Lizzie the 'Carnoustie lass' for example, his old nurse) and a sympathy with simple, passionate, honest and enduring people that cuts across every sort of snobbery and every pre-conceived opinion. He also has charm and – surprise, surprise for those who don't know how to read the novels – a sense of humour that is as often garish and larky as it is Timon-black. The variety and shades of humour are marvellously illustrated in one of the most entertaining bits of this collage, the telephone conversation with D (the stage designer Desmond Digby). The difficulty of integrating the campy, sardonic, spiky, morally uncompromising, vulnerable and self-parodying figure we are faced with here with the Great Author of, say, *The Aunt's Story* or *Riders in the Chariot*, is just what this unsettling confrontation with a contemporary is all about.

Scripsi, *1982*

ESCAPING THE CIRCLE OF HELL

THE BRITISH TEND TO think of Peter Porter as a resident Australian while recognising him as one of their finest poets. Australians, if the anthologists are any guide, do not know what to call him. He was born and grew up in Brisbane, left it finally when he was twenty-two, and has spent the whole of his working life in London. He makes no apology for being an expatriate. But where he writes from is not the heart of a lost empire but the heart of the language he speaks, which is, one suspects, the only place he has ever been at home.

Language is Porter's life as well as his livelihood. Reviewer, radio and film critic, record reviewer, and owner as he puts it in a poem of 'one hundred and seven Bach cantatas', lover of opera and Italy, occasional visitor to hell (his Brisbane childhood and adolescence provide as powerful a vision of it as Orcagna's), expert on the many ways of upsetting God's syllogism, he is a self-taught polymath, the cleverest poet since Auden when it comes to the apt allusion and the phrase that fixes in acid our late twentieth century in full cry – the cry often enough of rage and pain.

He is metropolitan, a born city-dweller: 'Where can there be nature enough,' he demands, 'to do without art?' Although he moves a bit awkwardly in the world of machines he is a post-technological man and finds room in his poems for everything our odd late world throws up. It is all grist to the mill of his dream-factory.

Porter knows more than most poets and uses what he knows. Our age is self-conscious: the world we inhabit is a vast museum – call it History, or Art, or the History of Art. For Porter, the exhibits are still alive and active. All those works by Melozzo da Forli or Piero di Cosimo or Giulio Romano, a lot of what happened in history (especially the darker bits, 'its truculent deeds of hate'), the operas of Donizetti, are still happening, right there in the daily life of the poems:

There was a sugar farmer's son (hyperthyroid)
I knew who was just like Nemorino,
And a girl at the Everest Milk Bar
Whose tits rubbed the cold of the ice-cream churn
As she reached down with her cheating scoop –
You saw more if you asked for strawberry –

She had a cold Christ hung over that defile
Crucified in silver, his apotheosis
In dry ice fumes. She was just like Bel' Adina
'Homage to Gaetano Donizetti'

After nearly forty years, given the openness of the poems and the wholeness of what he tries to grasp there, Porter's Australian experience may turn up at any moment. Most metaphors, as a late poem puts it, are 'home-produced', and poems are a place where time and tense have as little relevance as in dreams. In this sense, Porter never left Brisbane at all. In this sense too, he is, for all his eclecticism, as Australian as any of us. Which is only to assert that he is entirely himself:

Sparrows acclimatize, but I still seek
The permanently upright city where
Speech is nature and plants conceive in pots,
Where one escapes from what one is and who
One was, where home is just a postmark
And country wisdom clings to calendars.
The opposite of a sun-burned truth-teller's
World, haunted by precepts and the Pleides.
'On First Looking into Chapman's Hesiod'

That, thrown off with so much wit and flair, is an assertion, a cheeky one, of his right to be his own sort of poet and his own sort of Australian, an unrepentant stayer-away-from-home, whose being away makes 'home' an ambiguous but obsessive term in his work; like the life he escaped and the 'I' he evaded by going. It is one version – there are more than twenty million others – of what it means to be an Australian, and one example of how growing up Australian might hurt you into poetry and send you howling to your art.

'In the New World happiness is allowed,' a local reviewer asserts. Porter replies:

> No, in the New World, happiness is enforced.
> It leans your neck over the void and the only
> recourse is off to Europe . . .

The Australia Porter left in 1951 was a colonial backwater. Still recovering from two wars and the Great Depression, still lost in a dream of empire and half-living elsewhere, deeply puritanical and conservative, bellicosely anti-intellectual, it was the dull and decent place that some Australians now look back to with nostalgic regret; before migration and the various Libs. Most of all, before television, talk, Vietnam, cheap airfares and the Common Market changed us all for ever. It remains, for Porter, one of the circles of hell.

But if Martial got to Rome, and Gustav Mahler out

of his flea-ridden garrison town in Galicia (one of the 'poet-killing provinces'), why shouldn't a bright boy from Brisbane get to London and out of his Edwardian nightmare into the 1960s? Not all the barbarians who flocked to Rome were mercenaries and drunken louts. A few of them were bright young provincials who would one day be administrators, and some of them even emperors.

Porter has an affection for this version of London as late-imperial Rome; in one whole collection, he makes the Spanish-born satirist Martial his spokesman.

*

Late-imperial capitals are glittering assemblies of ex-colonials, deeply drawn to the dream of the ideal city and living in the real one with a mixture of contempt, disappointment, awe, gratitude for the escape it offers, anger at its cruelties, and sheer delight at the parade of follies it presents.

Lateness is essential to Porter's vision of the time he lives in. Anger and sadness; these are his mixed emotions, as the poems – their passion laced always with wit – mix satire and elegy. He does not always write from the Roman point of view, but the Roman experience is often there to provide a classic instance.

When Martial writes to his fellow-poet Juvenal back in Rome, ages and continents slide in and out

of one another like the double-exposure in some old
Hollywood film:

> . . . you're likely
> at this moment to be tramping round
> that speculator's mile, the loud Suburra
> where Empire ticks are sucking blood (called rental)
> from families, and young provincials slink
> home at evening clutching half a kipper;

> . . . I'm lazy
> here, a toff, I raise a spade just
> to let it fall (the Government stroke we say);
> I make friends in Boterdus and Platea
> (I give you two whole pentameters
> to laugh at these our Celtiberian names).
>
> 'After Martial', XII, XVIII

There is affection here for the outlandish 'other place',
as there is in 'On First Looking into Chapman's Hesiod'
for Boeotia and the kind of poet it produces, although
it is not the sort of poet Porter himself wants to be. The
poet he is, is remarkable.

Brisbane made him: so did his sullen after-life as
the latecomer in a late marriage, with 'a family tree
sited in hell; for whom the early lesson is "once bitten,
twice bitten" and "nothing crooked is made straight
and no rough places plain".'

His mother's death when he was nine made him. The sadness and guilt of it are in poem after poem.

His awful schooldays and his awful headmaster at Toowoomba made him, as described in 'Mister Roberts' and 'The View From Misfortune's Back'. That and the train-journeys home in 'carriages full of Glennie and Fairholme girls' – he 'the boy with something wrong reading a book'.

Reading books made him: Auden, Pope and Donne. So did music: Mozart (at twenty-one he could reel off all the Köchel numbers from K. 1 to K. 626), Donizetti, Verdi, Bruckner, those 107 Bach cantatas.

London and advertising made him, the frustration we see in 'John Marston Advises Anger' and the half-comic torments of getting a girl. Then marriage. Then Italy. Then the death of his wife, in which the sadness and guilt he so often turns to are brought to their highest pitch in a set of poems that stand at the very centre of his achievement and are some of the most passionate and moving works our century has produced.

Most of all, language made him. English – the complex, protean, hybrid, slangy, ever-inventive English of the late twentieth century that he moves in with so much dash and assurance, so much colonial cheek.

As for Australia – along with anthology pieces like 'Phar Lap in the Melbourne Museum', 'Sydney Cove', '1788' and the thread of childhood misery that runs through all his most personal poems, there is this. It is too disturbing a picture, and his own response to it too complex, for brief analysis. It is a picture we need to live with:

Here's a vision may be painted on a wall:
a man and a boy are eating with an Aborigine
in a boat, the sun turns up the tails of fish
lying beside the oars; the boy wipes surreptitiously
the bottle passed him by the black man.

Rain strums the library roof. The talk tonight
is 'Voluntary Euthanasia'. Trying to be classical
can break your heart. Depression long persisted in
becomes despair. Forgive me friends and relatives
for this unhappiness, I was away from home.
'In the New World Happiness Is Allowed'

Weekend Australian, 1988

A LAST FLING

THOMAS MANN BEGAN THE novel he would refer
to variously over the years as *The Confessions of a
Confidence Man*, *The Memoirs*, and finally *The
Confessions of Felix Krull, Confidence Man*, in 1909.
He was already, at thirty-four, the acclaimed author of
a dozen short stories or novellas, including one masterpiece, 'Tonio Kroger', and two novels, *Buddenbrooks*,
1901, and *Royal Highness*, 1909.

After the ease and assurance of *Buddenbrooks*, this
second novel had been slow in coming, and for all its
comic high jinks proved too knowingly self-conscious
to be much admired. In March 1910, Herman Hesse,
who was never really a friend, though he and Mann
did grow close in the years of their exile in the thirties,
had this to say of it:

It is only because we love and respect Thomas Mann

that we must take a severe view of his mannerisms. A lesser writer might make capital of the same tricks and subterfuges that irritate us in Mann, but it seems to us that an artist like Mann, whose intellect stands so high above all prejudices and delineates with such purity, ought in a seriously planned and seriously undertaken work, to dispense with this playing up to the public, witty and amusing as it may be, and whatever satisfactions he may derive from it. With such methods, unintentionally of course, he gives the average reader a certain sense of superiority but in turn cheats him out of all that's fine, serious and worth saying, for these things are said so softly and without emphasis that the average reader fails to notice them . . . A philistine can read this book and actually feel entertained . . . while subtlety after subtlety escapes him . . . We should like to read a book by Thomas Mann in which he doesn't think of the reader at all, in which he makes no attempt to seduce anyone or make anyone the butt of his irony. We shall never get such a book and our wish is unfair, for this cat and mouse game is essential to Mann . . .

This, coming from such a quarter, must have hurt. Hesse's evocation of the average or philistine reader would have hit home.

Mann took himself very seriously. Flattered as he had been by the success of *Buddenbrooks*, its popularity had also worried him. "'Am I so soft, so insipid, so mediocre," he had written to his Lubeck friend, Ida Boy-Ed, 'I have more than once asked myself, "that I should be loved like this?"' The mixture we get here of only half-hidden self-satisfaction and nagging self-doubt is just one of the ambiguities in Mann's complex nature that made him acutely sensitive to what his fellow writers, and a very alert and aggressive commentariat, thought of him.

Mann had seen himself from the beginning as the heir to Goethe, and like Goethe a darling of the Gods. But his assurance of being a chosen one was undercut by the fear that for all his natural talent, and his capacity for scholarship and hard work, he might not be recognised, in properly German terms, as a representative of the highest mind and thought. His formal education was limited. He had no academic qualifications. As a writer and thinker he was essentially self-taught.

Then there was the conflict he felt, as a son of conservative Lubeck, between his need on the one hand to maintain his status as a member of the high bourgeoisie – a worthy descendant of merchant forebears and himself a paterfamilias (in 1905 he had married into a rich family of Munich Jews, the Pringsheims) – and on the other hand his 'nature': an affinity with what he thought of as the irregular, the transgressive, the 'forbidden', and a suspicion, in line with the latest psychological thinking, that the many shifts and disguises that Eros and the erotic could assume, as perversity, or as illness, might be essential to what was most alive and personal in him, and to whatever authenticity he might lay claim to as an artist.

But however struck he may have been by Hesse's advice to 'desist from playing up to the public', he had already, in the new book he had embarked on, rejected it.

The Confessions is an *exercise* in seduction; the unapologetic apology, very direct and intimate, of a practised little poseur and flirt, who takes the reader warmly into his confidence (what else does it mean to be a 'confidence man'?), and, while openly admitting that he is a double-dealer – and even, yes, a thief – still takes it for granted that he will be forgiven, because he is such an engagingly witty and well-bred one: a creature of his own imagining, his own making, and a demonstration of the superiority of *spirit*, of what the French (Krull also of course has a good grasp of French) call *esprit*, over mere circumstance or *facts*.

Young Felix is the son of a Rhineland champagne-maker who is not above doctoring his product to lower the price. A high-school drop-out, a dreamer and devotee of what he calls 'The Great Joy' (mastur-bation), he is also an artist of a sort – the left-handed sort, a con-artist – very adroit at changing his costume, changing his story, changing his skin, and turning any situation he happens upon to his own advantage.

For Mann at his most playful and parodistic, Krull, another darling of the Gods, is his perfect surrogate and alter ego. This is Mann's sprightly portrait of the artist as showman, trickster, illusionist, in which the shameful facts of his own life are very cheekily transmuted and his darkest secrets, as he tells us, are on open view. A cat-and-mouse game indeed!

With its naked eroticism and joy in the 'forbidden', *Krull* was from the beginning the most confessional of Mann's books, a form of exuberant and liberating play; yet on three occasions over the years he set it aside, as if he had seen all along – or *it* did – that for all its heady youthfulness this was in the end to be a consolation of the author's unguarded and unbuttoned old age.

*

The earliest of these interruptions was in 1911 when Mann abandoned the *Confessions* for a story that had broken in on him all unexpectedly on a trip to Venice with his wife, Katya, and his brother Heinrich. This was the novella *Death in Venice*, which was to be a breakthrough work for Mann, one of the first clear masterpieces, in any language, of the new century. Then a year later, after a brief stay at a sanatorium at Davos, where Katya was undergoing treatment for TB, he was diverted a second time – briefly he thought – by an idea for a story that would be, as he tells us in a contemporary letter, 'a comic satyr's play to the tragic novel (*Death in Venice*) just written'. Mann was thinking of the satyr or goat's play that in the classic theatre restored an audience that had experienced the full range of pity and terror in *Oedipus* or *The Trojan Women* to the realm of the flesh, and sent them home purged a second time by Dionysian ribaldry and laughter.

As so often happened with Mann, the story grew under his hand as 'a whole world' revealed itself to him in what he calls 'a polyphony of themes': the body's power, through imagination or infection, to transform itself; forbidden (that is, homosexual) love; the lure of death; the education of his unlikely hero, the young Hamburg engineer, Hans Castorp, into 'the struggle for the new, after he has thoroughly savoured its components, Christianity and paganism'. (The important word here, given that it is Thomas Mann we are dealing with, is 'thoroughly'.)

Then, with so much in prospect but a pan-European catastrophe looming, this work too, 'The Magic Mountain' as he called it, was laid aside while he devoted himself – again briefly, as he thought – to an article on nationalism, the virtues of the military life and war. Except that the article too had a will of its own. As the war began and brutally unfolded, it too became a book in its own right, *The Reflections of an Unpolitical Man*, a vast work of over 500 pages that would occupy Mann for the next four years and lead him from his original position as a right-wing Nietzschian anti-democrat, through a whole rainbow of political opinions and affiliations – as anti-capitalist Social Democrat, uneasy Communist sympathiser and every point between – to his stance in the twenties as liberal pacifist and one of the leading supporters of the Weimar Republic. Meanwhile 'The Magic Mountain' joined *Felix Krull* in Mann's storage cupboard.

Then, on September 11th, 1918, with *The Reflections* already in the press, the Armistice about to be signed, the old Reich collapsing about him, and Munich, where he lived, on the way to becoming the capital of a Communist republic, Mann's thoughts returned to fiction: 'Will proceed to work,' he tells us in his Diaries, 'on the Magic Mountain [it was still at this point a novella] and the problem of its conclusion.'

In the event six months went by. Only on April 19th, 1919, does Mann note at last: 'After breakfast cleared my storage shelves somewhat, unpacked the manuscript of The Magic Mountain and took a look at the material'. Then, on April 30th: 'After an interval of four years began work again on The Magic Mountain.'

*

And *The Confidence Man?*

Some weeks earlier, on February 8th, Mann, in one of his many public readings, had given a performance of the school sickness chapter from *The Confidence Man*. He notes: 'This is perhaps the most remarkable thing I have ever written, but the book as a whole can hardly be kept at such a level.' Still it was not entirely out of his thoughts. On February 26th, he writes: 'How at home I always feel in the Goethean sphere; how it gladdens and stimulates me. If I manage to get back to *The Confidence Man*, I will be able to live and work entirely in that realm.' And he must have done so in the following months because two years later, on May 31st, 1921 he considers reading what he calls 'the military examination scene of Part II', which is where he stopped altogether and laid the work aside for what would be another thirty years.

Meanwhile, on November 14th, Mann notes in one of his precise Diary entries: 'Finished the fourth chapter of *The Magic Mountain* with the examination scene and Castorp's admission . . . I admit to myself that I have brought the book to the same point at which *The Confidence Man* came to a halt, and not by chance. Actually I have emptied my bag. Fiction must now take over. *Incipit ingenium*.'

What is interesting here is Mann's suggestion that the material of *The Confidence Man*, up to the point where it 'came to a halt', was also part of his 'bag'; had its sources, that is, in his own experience.

*

The military examination scene is an extension of the school sickness episode earlier in the book that Mann, when he read it some months before, had felt he could not surpass.

In that scene, young Felix, having learned as a lover and connoisseur of the body how, as he puts it, to 'parody nature' and make that wonderfully responsive organ obey his will, plays sick, and convinces the family physician, Health Councillor Dusing, by producing all the appropriate symptoms – a racing heart, high temperature, flushes – that he has a fever.

Five years later, called up now for military service, he ramps up his performance by producing the symptoms of an epileptic fit; all the while presenting himself as the very embodiment of patriotism, a youth passionate to do his duty, and insisting, to the consternation of the Surgeon General who is examining him, and despite what is clearly happening, that he is 'entirely fit for service'. In a piece of pure effrontery – and not only on Krull's part – Mann's cheeky hero, who has just cheated the army, and the nation, of his services, offers this very sophistical self-justification:

For though martial severity, self-discipline and danger had been the characteristics of my strange life, its primary prerequisite and basis has been freedom, a necessity completely irreconcilable with any kind of commitment to a grossly factual situation. Accordingly, if I lived *like* a soldier it would have been a silly misapprehension to believe that I should live *as* a soldier; yes, if it is possible to describe and define intellectually an emotional treasure as noble as freedom, then it may be said that to live like but not as a soldier, figuratively not literally, to be allowed to live symbolically, spells true freedom.

Mann, of course, knows perfectly well the cat-and-mouse game he is playing here, both with the elements of his own story and with motifs that elsewhere are 'sacred' to him: the motif of 'a soldier and brave' that is associated with Joachim Ziemssen in *The Magic Mountain*, his own wartime writings on the nobility of military service, the idea of 'representation' on which his public self and his role as a national figure is founded. Then there is his own rather doubtful relationship to the 'grossly factual'.

Mann, like Krull, had been a failure at school and had stayed on for a final year only to secure the elite status – which Krull lacks – of being a 'one-year recruit'. He presented himself for military service in 1901. He was twenty-six; with *Buddenbrooks* behind him but not yet established as a success, and in the midst of an emotional crisis, the last and most powerful of his 'adolescent' homosexual attachments, with Paul Ehrenberg. By a mixture of natural disadvantage (weak ankles), malingering, and a good deal of official string-pulling (nothing so dramatic or so virtuosic as Krull's imitation of a fit) he succeeded in getting himself honourably discharged, a fact that must have been a considerable embarrassment, a decade or more later, to so passionate a supporter of patriotic duty, military virtues and the War.

Krull's little performance allows Mann to rewrite all this in the spirit of subversive comedy, but also as a lighter version of the interaction between mind and body in the realm of disease that he was exploring, in all its disguises, and tricks, and misrepresentations, in *The Magic Mountain*.

*

A writer's body of work, if he is at all serious, has from first to last a coherence that may in the end be a mystery, even to himself. He can have no assurance when he begins that there will ever be such a thing as 'a body of work', and no clear notion, even as it emerges under his hand – slowly for the most part, and with many side-steps and interruptions – where it is taking him. First books for this reason have a double charm.

First there is their freshness, and what comes to us of a new voice and a new way of seeing; then there is what we catch when we go back with the writer's whole opus before us, and look again: the pre-echoes, sometimes faint, sometimes already strong, of what is to come, which the writing already had its sights on and was quietly pursuing.

In this longer view last works too have their special interest, and the more so when the writer sees himself as very deliberately bringing things to a conclusion; making an end. As Tolstoy did when, after three decades of devoting himself to moral tales, and works of educational and social reform, he returned, in *Hadji Murat*, to mere storytelling – as he puts it, 'like a greedy schoolboy going back for another slice of pudding' – and as Thomas Mann did in late 1950, when, after a lapse of almost thirty years, wearied after a near fatal encounter with lung cancer and in the disillusionment of his last months in America – after the long haul of *The Magic Mountain*, the four Joseph novels, his Goethe novel *Lotte in Weimar*, two novellas, *The Tables of the Law* and *The Transposed Heads*, the huge effort of *Dr Faustus* – he found himself returning to where, through all his years of exile, he had always been most at home. To 'the Goethean sphere' as he called it, the Greco-Goethean realm of open sensuality and intellectual play; of secret confession and unapologetic

325

affection for the egocentric self. To forbidden love. To 'dressing up' and 'fairytale magic' in the company of an adolescent charmer who, after so many years and so many delays and interruptions, was still waiting, in suspended animation, for his creator to catch up and offer him a second breath: the author's very own Happy One, Felix, a *drôle petit homme* who shifts very expertly, as occasion demands, from cringing subservience to inappropriate defiant hauteur, but is also magnanimous when it does him credit and no immediate harm, and for all his sensuality is also fastidiously restrained. A hotel lift-boy and toy-boy, who, half-educated as he is, has already learned the most useful of all lessons: that 'what we call fate is actually ourselves working through infallible laws'. A Sunday Child, and in his slim youth the latest and last incarnation – after Hans Hansen, Tadzio, Pribislav Hippe and the young Joseph – of what had always been the author's guiding deity: Hermes, lord of boundaries, god of liars, god of thieves.

Only with his body of honourable hard work behind him and his dignity as a public figure assured could the great novelist, at just on seventy-five, yield at last to his young seducer and give himself over to uninhibited invention.

What is extraordinary as we read on in *Krull* from the medical examination in Chapter 5 to the Paris Hotel chapters, 7 to 9, is the absence, after thirty years, of any perceptible break, either in invention or the comico-serious tone.

What Mann picks up on immediately is his narrator's optimistic openness – as at the beginning of a life, rather than its end; Krull's youthful delight in the sheer variety of what the world offers, in shop windows, a crowded hotel lobby, in human types and their accents, their physical tics and habits, in the clothes, ornaments, disguises they assume. All this, organised by Mann in his role as a latter-day Prospero, is a marionette dance, in which all his favourite motifs make a final, last-minute appearance – as in the liberation of old age, and the permissiveness of a later period – with a nod now to Genet rather than Gide – the great man himself does. In elegant drag as it happens, as a lady novelist of a certain age, Diane Philibert (Mme Houpflé, wife of a Strasbourg manufacturer of bathroom toilets), author of fictions as she puts it *'qui sont enormement intelligents'*, who never stops talking, even in orgasm, and admits to being, like her creator, an intellect that 'longs for the delights of the non-intelligent', that which is alive and beautiful *'dans sa stupidité'*.

Felix Krull lift-boy fits the bill perfectly, and she tells him so, delighted – though at twenty he is a little older than she would prefer – that he 'knows nothing of the alexandrine', and though he is himself a perfect Hermes, and even a real-life thief, has never heard of the god of so many shifts and disguises.

Krull, naturally, is not altogether pleased at being praised for his charming stupidity, but is happy to take what is at hand, including the invitation, after he has satisfied the lady's sexual needs, to creep about naked in the dark, and under the lady's direction locate and make off with her jewels.

Later, Mann makes a second and bolder appearance, as the discreetly homosexual and glumly self-repudiating Nectar, Lord Strathbogie, who falls for Krull (rather as Mann himself a little earlier had fallen for the nineteen-year-old waiter at his Swiss hotel, Franz Westermeier) and offers to recruit him as his body-servant and adoptive heir.

Felix delivers the dour Scotsman a severe admonition against self-repudiation, then very gently declines the proposal. 'This,' as he tells us of the promised ennoblement, 'would be a suspect lordship . . . But that was not the main thing. The main thing was that a confident instinct within me rebelled against a form of reality that was simply handed to me and was in addition sloppy – rebelled in favour of free play and dreams, self-created and self-sufficient, dependent, that is, wholly on imagination. When as a child I had woken up determined to be an eighteen-year-old prince named Karl and had maintained this pure and enchanting conceit for as long as I wished – that had been the right thing for me, not what this man with his jutting nose offered me because of his interest.'

The child who dreamed of being a prince named Karl, as we know from elsewhere, was Mann himself, as he was also the 'man with the jutting nose'.

*

In 1954, on the eve of his seventy-ninth birthday, and with *The Confessions of Felix Krull* about to be printed, Mann had second thoughts: 'not looking forward', he writes, 'to the publication of *Felix Krull*; the worst of it is that the whole thing strikes me as undignified nonsense, unlikely to impress the public with respect for an octogenarian'.

Mann need not have worried. *Krull* is well within the bounds of his oeuvre, a 'goat's play' to all the rest; a novel in the picaresque tradition of *Gil Blas* or Fielding's *Jonathan Wild*, of large scope and good cheer, that sends us back to Mann's earlier work with a new ear for the line of subversive comedy that he had always insisted was native to him but was obscured, for some of his readers, by the 'thoroughness' with which he develops his themes. (This was just one of the ways in which Mann felt, right to the end, that he was essentially misunderstood.) Krull, however wayward he may be on questions of honesty or truth, is never less than a perfect bourgeois when it comes to refinement and class.

*

For a work that really does run the risk of being identified as 'undignified nonsense', which is just what it sets out to be, we must go to Patrick White's *Memoirs of Many in One*, which stands in much the same relationship to *The Aunt's Story*, *The Tree of Man* and *Riders in the Chariot* in White's oeuvre as *Krull* does to *Death in Venice* and the Joseph books in Mann's. It too has its source in an unfinished fragment, or rather in two of them: a novella, 'Dolly Formosa's Last Stand', begun in 1966 and rapidly abandoned, and *The Binoculars of Helen Nell*, begun in 1964, put off while White wrote *The Solid Mandala*, taken up again in 1966, and finally laid aside, at 160,000 words, in 1967.

Slighter but more uninhibited than *Krull*, the product of a very different personality and a very different culture and time, *Memoirs* resembles Mann's comic masterpiece in being a work of travesty, an appendage, part Theatre of Cruelty, part Theatre of the Absurd, to the dozen or more weighty fictions that had won White his Nobel Prize. A whole range of White's earlier preoccupations, and provocations and types, are released here from their usual associations – anger, disappointment, outright disgust – and allowed to play up or run riot in the spirit of the London revue sketches that White had begun with in the early thirties, and whose influence, for all his 'grimness', he had never entirely thrown off. *Memoirs*, true to its English roots, is less a goat's play than a version of the jig with which an afternoon in the Elizabethan theatre with Timon or King Lear came to a conclusion in bawdy mayhem and the sprightliness of dance.

For White, as for Mann, writing was a form of dressing up, of acting out the various roles that haunted his true but hidden self. The desperate comedy of *Memoirs of Many in One*, if it is to be seen as White intended, has to be read as a burlesque version of all that he had devoted himself to in the five decades before. White describes what he was at in a letter of 1985: 'It's about premature senility. No. No. It's a very funny subject. It will offend a lot of people. Does them good. I enjoy it. It is religious in a sense; they won't like my approach to religion, the ones who are orthodox religious. And it's bawdy; the ones who like the bawdiness will be offended by the religion.'

The book purports to be the memoirs, edited by her friend, Patrick White (a local novelist and, in her eyes, failed artist) of Alex Xenophon Demirjian Gray, ex-nun, sometime actress, septuagenarian serial runaway, a Sydneysider but born in Alexandria and teetering now on the edge of senility – that is, if the fantasies and delusions she entertains us with are not in reality the last stages of true enlightenment.

Towards the end of the book Alex finds herself in a straitjacket, in the custody of a Colonel Superintendent and a 'bull-nosed' nurse. They decide to trust the old girl with another go at freedom, but not without conditions. 'Just you try to create, my girl,' the nurse warns her, 'and you'll be back in this before tea's up.'

White has always had an ear for the comic-sinister in Australian speech. 'Creating', playing up, is the essence of a life lived in the writing of it, as it is for her editor as well, though whether *this* Patrick White, who also happens to live at Centennial Park and wrestles with 'a growing stack of foolscap which he hopes will bring him fulfilment', is *our* Patrick White, is a matter of question.

Prissy, over-fastidious, fussily repressed, he bears an odd resemblance to one of White's least sympathetic but most pitiable characters, Waldo Brown of *The Solid Mandala*, who, while he is not quite an alter ego of his great creator, is in White's repertory of selves a clear admission of where, in another life and without the liberating plunge into 'creating', the piss-elegant and self-hating side of his divided nature might have taken him. As Alex sees it, 'Patrick understands the demands of art though he has never actually come good himself.' There are times in *Memoirs* where she is the one who bears a closer resemblance to *our* Patrick White than her dry-stick, uptight editor:

'I was sitting,' she tells us, 'in what I am vain enough to call my study, though I have studied practically nothing beyond my own intuition – oh, and by fits and starts, the Bible, the Talmud, the Jewish mystics, the Bhagavad Gita, various Zen masters, and dear old Father Jung who, I am told, I misinterpret.' And more vehemently later: 'Words are what matter. Even when they don't communicate. That's why I continue writing. Somebody may understand in time. All that I experienced on Nisos – as Cassini – in any of my lives, past and future – as Benedict, Magda, Dolly Formosa . . .'

If there is at the start of this narrative a clear line between narrator and editor, Alex and Patrick, it soon blurs. By the end of the book 'Patrick White's' Editor's Remarks have been invaded by Alex herself in the first person. She has, as White becomes Gray, entirely taken possession.

*

As the last work of a writer with a long and distinguished career, *Memoirs of Many in One* is not what some commentators would wish such a work to be; the noble culmination of all he can do. It was this sort of expectation that had worried Mann in the case of *Felix Krull*.

Memoirs, like *Krull*, is an escape from all that; a breaking free from the heavy burden that expectation sets on the writer's freer spirits; a return to what, for the writer himself, a Tolstoy, a Mann, a White, had always been at the core of his writing, a spirit of refreshment, of curiosity and discovery, of self-exploration in pure play.

For White, who comes to the moment later than the others, at a point of post-modernism that allows for a greater degree of permissiveness and different forms of play than Mann would have permitted himself, this becomes a test of his readers' capacity to read him, of the extent to which they have understood him, and, for those who meet the test, is meant to be a treat. Everything of White that they have previously encountered and taken in, from *The Aunt's Story*, through *Voss*, *Riders in the Chariot* and *The Solid Mandala* to *The Twyborn Affair* and *Flaws in the Glass*, makes a reappearance here, but in the form of conscious self-parody; most of all in a spirit of lightness in which the fearful, the terrible, but also the silliest and most foolish, find a place. We need, as readers, if we are to savour this as the treat White means it to be, to let go, as he does, of a good deal of baggage. To take on that lightness and feel the release of it. To kick up our heels and dance. To be capable, as readers, of entering whole-heartedly, as White does, into a jig. After so much suffering and pain, to grasp, as he does, and as he asks us to discover with him, the whole range of living, but also of the invigorating process by which the writing self takes life and makes of it the equally real but unpredictable other life we call Art.

INDEX